C
407.1
C 236
1997
GR 6-12

MYTHOLOGY

A Teaching Unit

Aileen M. Carroll

J. WESTON
WALCH
PUBLISHER
PORTLAND, MAINE

REPRODUCTION OF BLACKLINE MASTERS

These blackline masters are designed for individual student use and intended for reproduction by dry copier, liquid duplicating machine, or other means.

J. Weston Walch, Publisher, therefore transfers limited reproduction rights to the purchaser of these masters at the time of sale. These rights are granted only to a single classroom teacher, whether that teacher is the purchaser or the employee of a purchasing agent such as a school district. The masters may be reproduced in quantities sufficient for individual use by students under that teacher's direct classroom supervision.

Reproduction of these masters for use by other teachers or students is expressly prohibited and constitutes a violation of United States Copyright Law.

1   2   3   4   5   6   7   8   9   10

ISBN 0-8251-2871-4

Copyright © 1984, 1997
J. Weston Walch, Publisher
P.O. Box 658 • Portland, Maine 04104-0658

Printed in the United States of America

CONTENTS

FOREWORD

In presenting these lessons, the foremost objectives have been to show students that myths came into existence to fill a need, and to prove to students that myths still play an important role in our lives.

Some emphasis has been given to the practical reasons for studying mythology—to build vocabulary and increase understanding of figurative language in general and poetry in particular.

Since two stumbling blocks to learning mythology are the seemingly unpronounceable names of the characters and the bewildering array of conflicting stories, an easy-to-use pronunciation guide is provided. The stories are limited to the best known and most colorful, and therefore the easiest to remember.

Mythology: A Teaching Unit combines amusing activities such as the puzzle in Lesson 17 and the "classical classifieds" in Lesson 20 with more serious questions, which demand that the students reflect on what they have read, see parallels, and draw conclusions. While a special effort has been made to limit worksheet questions to the short-answer type, sometimes the nature of the question has made it necessary to require a longer answer.

The supplementary activities suggested for each lesson are designed to appeal to a variety of students, from those who want to do a brief oral report for extra credit to those with special literary or artistic ability who might want to get involved in a longer project. Individual students could volunteer to complete those activities that interest them.

Mythology provides a perfect bridge to other subjects, such as history, art, and music. Therefore, classes may want to go far beyond the activities suggested here. The possibilities for creative teaching of this subject are almost endless.

Whatever approach is chosen, students will be exposed to the oldest literature of the Western world, literature so imaginative and so thought-provoking that they are not apt to forget it.

TO THE TEACHER

Mythology: A Teaching Unit can be used effectively with students from middle school through high school age. However, you may want to use suggestions 2 and 3 below to tailor the units to your students' age and ability level.

SUGGESTIONS

1. Because the lessons are developed sequentially, students should keep all lessons and completed worksheets in a folder or loose-leaf notebook so that they can refer to them easily. You will note, however, that the text is divided into three parts, each with its own final test. Therefore, you may use all three or only the ones that you believe hold special interest for your students.

2. Many of the worksheets are designed to help the students see parallels and draw conclusions on their own. If you are working with younger students, however, Lessons 12, 14, 19, 23, 25, 30, 32, and 33 might make a more lasting impression, and the students might draw sounder conclusions if a class discussion preceded their completing of the worksheets. Suggestions for presenting each of these lessons are in the Teacher's Ready Reference.

3. The study of mythology is an easy way for students to improve their vocabularies. Words and expressions derived from mythological sources are presented throughout the unit. The lessons can also serve as a means of increasing students' general vocabulary. In the Ready Reference are included words that students might need to review with you before they read each lesson. (If no vocabulary words are shown for a particular lesson in the Ready Reference, special emphasis has been given to vocabulary on the worksheets.) Another possibility is to review the words with the students as soon as they have read the lesson so that you can determine whether they understood the words from context.

4. Suggested activities and answers to the worksheet questions are included in the Ready Reference for each lesson.

TEACHER'S READY REFERENCE

LESSON 1

VOCABULARY FOR REVIEW

speculate   forbade   awe   reverent

SUPPLEMENTARY ACTIVITIES

A. Imagine you are a person from ancient times entering a railroad or highway tunnel for the first time. Write a myth to explain the existence of the tunnel.
B. Imagine that you, one of the ancients, are present at the launching of a space shuttle. Write a mythic explanation of the event.

ANSWER KEY

1. B; C; teaches that the child should obey the parent and that the young should heed good advice; also teaches that human beings must not try to act like gods, i.e., "fly too high"
2. A; explains the change of seasons
3. B; C; teaches obedience to authority and that it is impossible to cheat death

VOCABULARY

1. cereal
2. comes from Orpheus, the divine musician

LESSON 2

VOCABULARY FOR REVIEW

chronological   vulnerable
arachnid   fantastic (gives meaning other than current slang)

SUPPLEMENTARY ACTIVITIES

A. Make a collection of ads with mythological connections, to be used on the bulletin board. Example: Ajax cleanser.
B. Find mythic references on the sports page of the newspaper and bring them in for the bulletin board. Example: He showed herculean strength.

ANSWER KEY

Order may vary, but pairing is as follows: Venus, doves, A; hawks, B; cereal, C; corn goddess, D; Achilles, E; Ajax, F; chronological, G; arachnids, H; wings on your feet, Mercury, I; Nike, J; Panasonic, K.

LESSON 3

You may want to hold a class discussion on the subject of altruism and moral courage.

VOCABULARY FOR REVIEW

crafty   persistence

SUPPLEMENTARY ACTIVITIES

In a short report, compare a real modern hero with an ancient mythical hero.
Example: Compare a heavyweight boxing champion with Hercules.

ANSWER KEY

1. He was a self-made man who also worked to help others.
2. She showed willingness to sacrifice her own comfort to save others, determination, and the will to win against great odds.
3. Kennedy was seen as attempting to create an ideal world, as did Arthur.
4. She was a self-made woman.
5. Both require physical courage, leadership, the will to win over obstacles. The game is a combat for territory.

LESSON 4

You will want to give students a brief account of the Trojan War, including the story of the Trojan Horse, before they do the worksheet.

VOCABULARY FOR REVIEW

row   defy

SUPPLEMENTARY ACTIVITIES

Search your school's art print collection, art reference books, and mythological encyclopedias for reproductions of famous paintings inspired by myths, and bring them to class. Examples: Sargent's *Hercules Kills the Hydra*; Botticelli's *Birth of Venus*, or *Mars and Venus*; Rubens's *Vulcan at His Smithy*.

ANSWER KEY

1. Apollo
2. Apollo, sky or heavens
3. sky
4. early morning
5. Answers will vary (buttercup, tulip)
9. Daedalus and Icarus
10. Icarus flew too close to the sun and lost his life.
11. a poet of ancient Greece
12. the Trojan War
13. Answers will vary.

LESSON 5

VOCABULARY FOR REVIEW

meditation

SUPPLEMENTARY ACTIVITIES

Make a collection of trademarks or emblems with mythological associations to be used on the bulletin board. Example: Mercury as the symbol of the Florists' Transworld Delivery Association.

ANSWER KEY

H, D, J, A and F, C, E, B,G, I

LESSON 6

You might tell students that they will meet each of the following again and learn more about their stories: Europa, Woden, Uranus, Daphne, Pandora.

VOCABULARY FOR REVIEW

solstice   irrational

SUPPLEMENTARY ACTIVITIES

Enlarge your vocabulary by making a collection in your loose-leaf notebook of words from the myths.

ANSWER KEY

1. atlas
2. chronological
3. geography
4. martial
5. atrophy
6. cereal
7. arachnids
8. phobia
9. panic
10. pandemonium
11. pantheist
12. syringe
13. plutonium
14. lethal
15. cloth
16. erotic
17. odyssey
18. Junoesque
19. herculean
20. mercurial
21. Jovian
22. Orpheum

LESSON 7

VOCABULARY FOR REVIEW

assumption   principle   multilate   fanciful

SUPPLEMENTARY ACTIVITIES

Find and read an American Indian creation myth, preferably from your section of the country. Make an oral report to the class.

ANSWER KEY

1–4. chronological, chronology, chronometer, geographic, geography, geophysics, erotic, erotica, chaotic, chaotically
5. In the case of the ship or the missile, each is large and powerful. The business titan has achieved power.
6. from Gaea, as the first mother from whom all else sprang
7. Probably governments changed as more powerful figures came onto the scene and deposed or killed the old rulers.

LESSON 8

VOCABULARY FOR REVIEW

enlist   grudge   depose   deception

SUPPLEMENTARY ACTIVITIES

If you enjoyed "leafing out" the gods' family tree, you might like to make a poster board chart for Zeus and his family. As you continue studying the myths, you will find that he had many children. A good mythological dictionary will list, under his name, his children and their mothers.

ANSWER KEY

1. Chaos
2. Rhea
3. Nyx
4. Uranus
5. Hades
6. Eros
7. Zeus
8. Cronus
9. Erebus
10. Poseidon
11. Gaea

LESSON 9

VOCABULARY FOR REVIEW

disgorge   exemplary   relentless   domain
wrath   custodian   endow   scepter
doomed

SUPPLEMENTARY ACTIVITIES

A. Find a detailed account of Athena's unusual birth. Decide what is revealed about Zeus's character in this myth. Report your findings to the class.
B. Find an account of how Athens was named. Why didn't the people choose Poseidon instead of Athena as their patron? Report to the class.

ANSWER KEY

C, O, A, K, B, D, F, G, J, I, H, P, L, N, E, M

LESSON 10

VOCABULARY FOR REVIEW

vindictive   blight

SUPPLEMENTARY ACTIVITIES

Find an account of Artemis's treatment of Actaeon. Was her action justified? Tell the story and your opinion of the goddess's behavior to the class.

ANSWER KEY

A. moonstruck: dazed or crazed; from Artemis, goddess of the moon, who could drive people insane
B. brainchild: a product of thought; from Athena, goddess of wisdom, child of Zeus's brain
C. aphrodisiac: stimulating love or desire; from Aphrodite, goddess of love
D. from hundred-eyed Argus, who could see, and therefore knew, everything
E. from proud Hera, whose bird was the peacock
F. Hera
G. Aphrodite

LESSON 11

You may want to describe the gods' home and activities on Olympus to the students after they read the lesson.

VOCABULARY FOR REVIEW

oratory	frenzied	oracle	bloodthirsty
esteem	redeeming	resurrection	vagabond

SUPPLEMENTARY ACTIVITIES

A. Look up the story of Zeus and Semele to find the details of Dionysus's birth. Report to the class.
B. In an art reference book or a mythological encyclopedia, find pictures of the *Apollo Belvedere* and the *Hermes of Praxiteles*. Bring them to class.

ANSWER KEY

1. acrophobia
2. claustrophobia
3. orgy
4. lyric
5. panic
6. phobia
7. hydrophobia
8. satyrs
9. The Greeks admired Apollo and Athena for their wisdom and their rational behavior.

LESSON 12

To give the students a better understanding of the Greek attitude toward the "average woman," a discussion contrasting Pandora and Athena would be useful. In preparation for the final worksheet question, it may be necessary that the students see Athena as atypical of the Greek concept of womanhood since the myths about her emphasize her intellect, her apparent disdain for emotional involvement, and her warlike qualities.

VOCABULARY FOR REVIEW

dominion   deceitful   vengeful   celestial
foresight

SUPPLEMENTARY ACTIVITIES

Find the story of Cupid and Psyche. Psyche went down to the Underworld to get a famous urn or box. Is there any similarity between her story and the story of Pandora's box? Report to the class.

ANSWER KEY

1. steal, disobeyed or defied
2. foresee, feared
3. foresight, good or sound
4. disobedience, curiosity
5. Eve and the apple
6. Yes, hope remained for human beings.

LESSON 13

VOCABULARY FOR REVIEW

ruthless   ingenious   susceptible   nymph
infatuated

SUPPLEMENTARY ACTIVITIES

In an astronomy book, find a picture of the constellation Orion. Then list any other constellations whose names you recognize from the myths you have read. Report to the class.

ANSWER KEY

2, 3, 9, 16, 4, 5, 13, 10, 1, 8, 12, 11, 6, 7, 17, 18, 19, 20, 14, 15

LESSON 14

Some discussion of the parallels may be necessary to prepare the students for the worksheet. They need to see Deucalion and Pyrrha as the parents of a new race. They also should see the parallel to the story of Noah and the Ark.

VOCABULARY FOR REVIEW

memento   deluge   lax   guise

SUPPLEMENTARY ACTIVITIES

Using Bulfinch's *Mythology* or a similar reference, find the story of each of the following and report it to the class.

Philemon and Baucis (Students should see parallel.)

Cadmus and the sowing of the dragon's teeth

ANSWER KEY

1. She, too, became the mother of the race.
2. Noah and the Ark
3. to explain a natural phenomenon and to point out a moral (People had not been reverent to the gods.)
4–5. Answers will vary.

LESSON 15

VOCABULARY FOR REVIEW

rashly   evolve   dissuade   incessant
gadfly

SUPPLEMENTARY ACTIVITIES

Try writing a myth in which you explain some natural phenomenon, for example, a rainbow.

ANSWER KEY

1. overconfidence
2. Icarus
3. vegetation
4. color
5. pride, overconfidence
6. fly up to heaven
7. tendency to talk too much
8. in love with himself
9. Students can relate this to the stories of Icarus, Bellerophon, or Phaeton.

LESSON 16

SUPPLEMENTARY ACTIVITIES

With poster board, use your original drawings or take cutouts from magazines to make an illustrated map of Hades. Be sure to include such characters as Tantalus and Sisyphus.

ANSWER KEY

1. Answers will vary.
2. It was best to be a hero.
3. Hades was the god of the Underworld, but unlike Satan, he did not give out any punishments.
4. dictionary work

LESSON 17

VOCABULARY FOR REVIEW

pitfall

SUPPLEMENTARY ACTIVITIES

In a mythological reference book (or encyclopedia or dictionary), find Tiresias's story. It's an unusual one.

Read the story of Agamemnon. How did his wife betray him? Make oral reports of your findings.

ANSWER KEY

Faces and places in Hades's Realm

1. faces	8. Dis	15. Ixion	21. Semele
2. Aeacus	9. Phlegethon	16. Neoptolemus	22. Rhadamanthus
3. Charon	10. Lethe	17. Hades	23. Eurydice
4. Eurydice	11. Agamemnon	18. Acheron	24. Achilles
5. Sisyphus	12. Cerberus	19. Dionysis	25. Lethe
6. Anticleia	13. Elpenor	20. Elysian Fields	26. Minos
7. Neoptolemus	14. Styx		

LESSON 18

VOCABULARY FOR REVIEW

harassment   centaur   atonement

SUPPLEMENTARY ACTIVITIES

A. Find a list of all twelve labors of Hercules. Which seems most difficult to you? Why? What qualities of a hero does Hercules display in any two of the labors? Write a brief report answering these questions.

B. Read an account of Paul Bunyan's exploits. Report to the class.

C. Find out what you can about the real man John Henry. Report to the class.

ANSWER KEY

1. A. brave, willing to face the unknown
    B. brave, willing to face the unknown
    C. accomplished great feats of strength
2. Hercules, from his lion tunic
    Achilles, from his dip in the Styx
3–4. Answers will vary.

LESSON 19

Some review of just how Ariadne, Danaë, and Andromeda were treated might be useful before the students complete the worksheet.

VOCABULARY FOR REVIEW

labyrinth

SUPPLEMENTARY ACTIVITIES

Find the story of another ancient hero, Jason, and his quest for the Golden Fleece. Relate the story to the class, comparing Jason with Perseus and Theseus wherever possible.

ANSWER KEY

1. C	4. B	6. E	9. Answers will vary.
2. A	5. C	7. F	10. Students should realize that woman
3. E and G	6. E	8. C	were not held in high esteem.

LESSON 20

You may want to have students read the Cyclops story, or relate it to them as an example of Odysseus's cleverness and impulsiveness.

VOCABULARY FOR REVIEW

invulnerable	retaliate	taunt	appease
tribulations	foolhardy		

SUPPLEMENTARY ACTIVITIES

In a mythological dictionary or encyclopedia, find out what you can about the Trojan hero Hector. Then, in a short paper, compare him with Achilles and/or Odysseus. Which hero do you prefer? Why?

ANSWER KEY

1. Andromeda	5. Danaë	9. Theseus	13. Graiai
2. Minos	6. Ariadne	10. Sirens	14. Polyphemos
3. Augeas	7. Odysseus	11. Penelope	15. Perseus
4. Thetis	8. Tiresias	12. Perseus	

LESSON 21

VOCABULARY FOR REVIEW

deity	counterpart

SUPPLEMENTARY ACTIVITIES

A. Find out more about the lives of the Vestal Virgins. Report to the class. Find the story of Romulus and Remus. Report to the class.

B. Using reference books on art or mythology, find pictures of both Greek and Roman statues of the major gods. Can you see any differences in the way the Greek and the Roman sculptors portrayed their subjects?

ANSWER KEY

1. Janus	7. Mercury	13. Vulcan	19. Mars
2. Vesta	8. Apollo	14. Pluto	20. Janus
3. Ceres	9. Janus	15. Neptune	21. Jupiter
4. Jupiter	10. Diana	16. Mercury	22. Mercury
5. Juno	11. Minerva	17. Mercury	23. Mars
6. Bacchus	12. Mars	18. Mercury	24. Juno

LESSON 22

SUPPLEMENTARY ACTIVITIES

A. Divide the class according to zodiac signs—all Leos together, all Capricorns together, etc. Ask them to do library research to find the characteristics of those born under their particular sign and to report to the class on their research. Individuals within each group might also like to discuss with each other how well they fit the zodiacal description of their character.

B. Several students could consult a dictionary of symbols to find out more about the magical number twelve (Seven and Three are also magical numbers.) Remind them of the Twelve Labors of Hercules. Ask them to discover other significant groups of twelve.

ANSWER KEY

1–3. Answers will vary.

4. Answers will vary, but microscope, stethoscope, and periscope are a few.

5. Cassius believes we make our own destiny; we shouldn't blame the stars. Shakespeare is expressing the Renaissance point of view.

6. The planets move, or wander.

LESSON 23

The students need to realize that since the ancients had no good means of controlling the weather—at least, we can control indoor temperature—the cold in a northern area such as the land of the Norsemen was a life-threatening force. thus the frost giants, as a symbol of that weather, would seem especially menacing.

VOCABULARY FOR REVIEW

lowering   gnome   reincarnate

SUPPLEMENTARY ACTIVITIES

With poster board, make a drawing of the Norse universe. Be sure to include Yggdrasil and show that its roots are in several regions.

ANSWER KEY

1. Thetis
2. Achilles
3. Elysian Fields
4. Snow and cold posed a real threat to the Norse.
5. The land was cold. The hours of daylight in winter were short.
6. Answers will vary.
7. It was generally gloomy and pessimistic.

LESSON 24

SUPPLEMENTARY ACTIVITIES

Create your own tree of life. Draw a large tree with its roots showing. On the roots, write the names of your four grandparents. If you put your father's parents on the left, write the names of their children on the lowest left branch. Do the same thing for your mother's parents and their children on the right branch. Then write you r father's and your mother's full name again on the trunk of the tree. On the left branch above them write your brothers' names and on the right branch write your sisters' names. Then put your own name again on the trunk just above those branches. you now have the beginning of a family tree.

ANSWER KEY

1. impale
2. siege
3. annihilation
4. banished
5. runes
6. Athena
7. Answers will vary. Both are strong and long-lived.
8. ghosts of Christmas Past, Present, and Future

LESSON 25

Before the students complete this worksheet, a class discussion could bring out the new emphasis in the medieval tales on such qualities as selflessness, consideration for others, modesty, and chastity.

VOCABULARY FOR REVIEW

exploit   subdue   foster (son)   mortal (as an adjective)

SUPPLEMENTARY ACTIVITY

Read in T.H. White's novel *The Once and Future King*, the account of Arthur's (Wart's) pulling of the sword from the stone. Describe its details to the class.

ANSWER KEY

1. unselfish
2. Beowulf battles for others' sake; Odysseus battles for himself. Beowulf is selfless.
3. He is chaste, pure.
4. modest
5–6. Answers will vary.

LESSON 26

ANSWER KEY

8, 11, 12, 1, 2, 4, 14, 13, 9, 7, 6, 10, 3, 5, 15

16–18. All three can be called allusions, but 17 is also a simile and 18 a metaphor.

19. Midas turned everything to gold.
20. The owl symbolizes knowledge and wisdom.
21. Pegasus, the flying horse, symbolizes power and speed.
22. just and paternal
23. relentless and restless
24. mysterious and gloomy
25. jealous and vain
26. beautiful and unfaithful
27. wise and warlike
28. youthful and unpredictable
29. reasonable and health-giving
30. bloodthirsty and fickle
31. It gave people an advantage over all other animals.
32. laurel tree
33. promise to marry him
34. People had been wicked or people no longer respected the gods.
35. listen to advice and obey his or her elders
36. Christ
37. evil
38. Norns, or Fates
39. eyes; spring
40. tremble
41. doomsday
42. insects; dragon

LESSON 27

VOCABULARY FOR REVIEW

| counterpart | embellish | inundate | revere |
| embalm | fearsome | | |

SUPPLEMENTARY ACTIVITIES

A. Have students a sketch either Bast, the cat goddess, or Anubis, the jackal-headed god.
B. Three people can draw Amam, the devourer, in three sections. Each team member needs a piece of graph paper on which to draw one section of Amam. The person drawing the head and forequarters should sketch on the right side of the paper. The person drawing the body should extend it from one side of the paper to the other. The person drawing the hindquarters should draw on the left side of the paper. Put the three sheets together and you have an animal drawn by committee.

ANSWER KEY

1. 1000
2. animals and half-animal/half-human creatures
3. different storytellers and different names in different parts of Egypt
4. punishable by death

5. scarab beetle was worshipped
6. flooding of the Nile
7. resurrection
8. jackal follows predators and eats carrion

LESSON 28

SUPPEMENTARY ACTIVITIES

A. Have students look in an encyclopedia of mythology to find out more about Isis's wanderings while she searched for Osiris. Ask them to report to the class.

B. Have students look up the story of Horus's battle with his uncle Set and his ruthlessness toward his mother when she took pity on Set. In class discussion, ask if Horus was a hero or a villain. Does he fit the pattern of earlier heroes the class has met in the myths?

ANSWER KEY

1. A. Ra;   B. Geb
2. A. Isis;   B. Set
3. A. Isis;   B. Set;   C. Horus
4. Compensation
5. Extremely wicked

6. causing trouble or worry to another repeatedly
7. one who sues in a court of law
8. to proceed against judicially
9. Isis, Osiris, and Horus

LESSON 29

VOCABULARY FOR REVIEW

incantation   perpetual   prey

SUPPEMENTARY ACTIVITIES

A. In an encyclopedia of mythology or of Egyptian mythology, find examples of Egyptian art—friezes, urns, etc. Photocopy them and mount them on poster board for classroom display. In class discussion, ask students to point out differences between the sculpture of Greece and Rome and the art of Egypt.

B. As an enrichment project, show the video *Antony and Cleopatra*, filmed in 1973. Students will enjoy the love story. Ask them to pay special attention to backgrounds and see if they can discover anything that is significant to them because they have had this brief look at Egyptian mythology.

ANSWER KEY

1. in the sky, away from the gods' dwelling place, above the earth
2. mountain ranges and a river
3. demons and fierce animals

4. warnings about the demons and fierce beasts, especially Amam
5. *Book of the Dead*
6. Kingdom of Osiris
7. purgatory, where souls atoned for sins

LESSON 30

VOCABULARY FOR REVIEW

antiquity   chaos   orifice

SUPPLEMENTARY ACTIVITIES

A. Have students look in an encyclopedia for a brief description of Taoism and report about it to the class.
B. Have students draw a cartoon of sky, earth, and P'an Ku stretched out between them. Tell them to give sky and earth faces if they wish, and to include the horns that grew from P'an Ku's forehead and the tusks that protruded from his mouth.

ANSWER KEY

1. Chaos had to be destroyed and order accomplished.
2. that individuals were insignificant; not even as important as mud or fleas.
3. Each died to create the world.
4. yin: female, darkness, earth, negative, cold
   yang: male, light, sky, positive, heat

LESSON 31

VOCABULARY FOR REVIEW

decoy   embody   regenerate   renaissance
elusive   feat

SUPPLEMENTARY ACTIVITIES

A. Read "Jabberwocky," by Lewis Carroll, to the class and distribute photocopies. Ask a volunteer or volunteers to try to draw a Jabberwocky on the chalkboard, using details from the poem.
B. Try to assemble a classroom collection of items that show unicorns.
C. In class discussion, ask students where the concept of a dragon or a unicorn may have come from. Record the various theories on the chalkboard and take a vote as to which explanation is most plausible.

ANSWER KEY

1. C; 2. D; 3. G; 4. D; 5. A; 6. C; 7. G; 8. D; 9–13. B; 14. F; 15. E;

16. Bigfoot and the Loch Ness monster

LESSON 32

SUPPLEMENTARY ACTIVITIES

A. From encyclopedias, books about Chinese mythology, or books about the decorative arts, find examples of Chinese-decorated earthenware or porcelain plates, fans, screens, clothing, etc. Photocopy the illustrations and arrange them as a bulletin board display. Look especially for scenes from the myths, sometimes used on plates.

B. Have students look in an encyclopedia and read about the Chinese respect for the elderly and reverence for the dead. Have them report to the class.

ANSWER KEY

1. position, character
2. made a god
3. meeting of spiritualists to receive spirit communication
4. wizard
5. depending on the will or pleasure of others
6. a show of magnificence
7. a large kettle
8. Her mercy and compassion
9. Interested in money, wealth
10. Inferior to males; the answer was "not good" if an unborn child's gender was female.
11. Divination

LESSON 33

SUPPLEMENTARY ACTIVITIES

A. (*For older students*) Ask a small group to study William Wordsworth's "Intimations of Immortality" and then to present it to the class, putting special emphasis on the verse that begins "Our birth is but a sleep and a forgetting." Pass out photocopies of the poem. Ask the class if they can see how the poem could be related to this lesson. *Hint:* Remember that Hindu belief seems to assure reincarnation.

B. Ask students to find an account of Siva's love life in a book of Hindu mythology and have them report to the class. (Siva had more than one wife.)

ANSWER KEY

1. prematurely
2. assimilating
3. custom
4. rituals
5. ascetic
6. manifestation
7. It was necessary to remove all the dead creatures and plants.
8. Apparently, people would not need to atone; they would simply be reincarnated.
9. reincarnation
10. the prime mover, god

LESSON 34

VOCABULARY FOR REVIEW

caste   compassion   purge   self-denial
circumvent   ethical

SUPPLEMENTARY ACTIVITY

A. In an encyclopedia, find the actual rules or precepts that Buddha laid down in his eightfold path. Read them to the class and discuss how each one would benefit the individual and other people.

B. (*For older students*) Ask students to find a copy of William Butler Yeats's poem "Sailing to Byzantium." Let them discuss it in small groups to be sure that they understand it. Have a volunteer read it to the class and distribute photocopies. In class discussion, relate Yeats's attitude in stanzas 3 and 4 to the attitude of the ascetics in today's lesson who long to free themselves of earthly desires. Ask students if they see the connection.

ANSWER KEY

1. H; 2. I; 3. B and K; 4. A; 5. E; 6. J; 7. F; 8. D; 9. G; 10. C

LESSON 35

A. 3; B. 11; C. 4; D. 1; E. 5; F. 7; G. 9; H. 2; I. 10; J. 8; K. 12; L. 6; M. 14; N.13; O. 15

16. The phoenix rose from the ashes.
17. The tiger was the king of the beasts—the top.
18. pomp
19. manifestation
20. orifices

21. heinous
22. attributes
23. animal
24. water; egg
25. life
26. Christ's death and resurrection

LESSON 36

VOCABULARY FOR REVIEW

cannibalism   renowned   ruthless   wizard
fossil

SUPPLEMENTARY ACTIVITIES

A. In a handbook of literary terms or in an encyclopedia, find out the meaning of the term "beast fable." Report your findings to the class. A small group might read one or two of Aesop's Fables and then present them to the class, taking on the roles of the animals in the stories.

B. Anyone who has read *Animal Farm* might give a brief summary to the class, explaining that animals are used to show failings that are really human failings.

ANSWER KEY

1. Answers will vary.
2. A. fetish to bring good luck
3. Answers will vary.
4. A worry stone is supposed to soothe the person who carries it and strokes it when nervous.
5. Answers will vary.
6. Northwest
7. a time of famine
8. Answers will vary.
9. We can assume that the hare and hyena are young and that the mothers are old and have already lived a long time.
10. Answers will vary.

LESSON 37

SUPPLEMENTARY ACTIVITIES

Photocopy and enlarge an outline map of Africa. Mount it on poster board for classroom display. Students should break up into groups of three or four, with each group responsible for some kind of illustration of one of the following:

the myth of Number Eleven—Ghana   the myth of the spider Anansi—
the myth of Nkoyo—Nigeria   Sierra Leone, Ghana
animal gods—Sudan and Ethiopia

Place the illustrations on the map in the proper geographic location.

ANSWER KEY

1. (c),   2. (d),   3. (a),   4. (b),   5. (d),   6. (c),   7. (b)

8. In each, the main character returns from the dead.
9. Children should obey their parents. Also, things are not always what they seem.
10. Number Eleven is clever enough to outsmart his mother and anyone else who stands in the way of his survival.

LESSON 38

VOCABULARY FOR REVIEW

benefactor   gluttonous   realm

SUPPLEMENTARY ACTIVITIES

A. Find a map of the United States that shows where the various tribes of Native Americans lived. Photocopy it for the bulletin board. Check the *National Geographic* or *American Heritage* index to find such a map.
B. On the chalkboard, make a list of words we've inherited from the Indians, for example, *tepee, wigwam, wangan, calumet, wampum,* etc.

C. Make a second list of proper names from the Indians, for example, Lake Huron, Passamaquoddy Bay, Winnebago R.V., Pontiac automobile. Try to add to these lists daily as you study this unit.

ANSWER KEY

1. muskrat
2. Raven
3. coot
4. Grandmother Spider
5. Buzzard
6. Possum
7. daughter of Chief-Who-Had-Light,
8. Great Horned Snakes
9. Thunderbirds
10. All Spirit,
11. Great Hare
12. Raven
13. Grandmother Earth
14. His quills are like rays; the bear is dark and threatening.
15. Answers will vary.

LESSON 39

SUPPLEMENTARY ACTIVITIES

A. Find a copy of *The Algonquin Legends of New England* or a similar collection of Indian myths and legends. Read more about Glooskap's remarkable exploits and report to the class.
B. Several students could work together selecting portions of Longfellow's *Hiawatha* to present to the class, making their readings as dramatic as possible.
C. The Wabanaki, Micmacs, and Maliseets were all part of the Algonquin nation. Read more about these tribes to see exactly where they lived. Use a map of the Northeast to show the class what you found out.

ANSWER KEY

1. One bad person can spoil things for everyone else.
2. She saw them in a physical sense, but she also saw what they were really like.
3. Mrs. Bear was physically stronger.
4. Because it was isolated, Lox may have singled it out. Also, because no other villagers were near, there were no witnesses to the "other" woman's selfishness.
5. guileless: innocent
   credulous: inclined to believe
   gullible: easily fooled or imposed upon
   naive: unsophisticated, artless
   Answers will vary.

LESSON 40

VOCABULARY FOR REVIEW

boon	courage	endurance	thong
bravery			

SUPPLEMENTARY ACTIVITIES

A. In your school library, find a copy of Stephen Vincent Benet's short story "By the Waters of Babylon" and use it for an in-class reading assignment with each student reading a section aloud. As you will see, the story is really a myth set in the future.

B. In a class discussion, first determine what the story has in common with the myth about how the Indians discovered corn. Then try to imagine what would happen if an Indian during his fast had a vision of our world today. What might he find amazing? What would probably earn his disapproval?

ANSWER KEY

1–4. Answers will vary.
   5. The most likely one is sports
   6. Answers will vary.

LESSON 41

VOCABULARY FOR REVIEW

impiety   plague   spawning season   teem
malady

SUPPLEMENTARY ACTIVITY

In the legend, the Camas probably corrected some deficiency in the Indians' diet. The Indians had a remarkable collection of cures. Check your library for a book describing Indian remedies and report to the class. (Some of those remedies were adopted by the early settlers, and some are still in use today.)

ANSWER KEY

1. is a woman
2. God
3. purity
4. possibly scurvy from lack of Vitamin C
5. Medicine men's prayers were answered; people later offered sacrifices.
6. They only killed the salmon they needed to survive.
7. They became lazy and undisciplined because their lives were too "easy."
8. volcanic eruption

LESSON 42

SUPPLEMENTARY ACTIVITIES

In the library, try to find pictures of Spider Rock and of the cliff dwellings made by the Indians of the Southwest. Bring the pictures to class to share with the group. If you are artistic, try drawing a picture of Spider Woman for the bulletin board. More than one student could do this project. In the classroom, two students could pantomime the scene of the young Indian, his pursuer, and the climb up the face of the cliff.

ANSWER KEY

1. insatiable
2. retrieve
3. entice
4. refuge
5. climbing the rock.

6. He doesn't seem to be brave.
7. A woman should not try to take a man's place.
8. Answers will vary.
9. kindness and respect

LESSON 43

FINAL TEST

1, 3, 4, 12, 14, 2, 5, 7, 6, 11, 8, 9, 10, 13

15. gain the animal's strength and protection
16. respected them
17. wouldn't accept her father's judgment and choice of suitors
18. A woman should not try to take on a man's job.
19. She is too trusting.

20. She is selfish.
21. to prove his manhood
22. impiety
23. voracious
24. ingenuity
25. gullible
26. entice

LESSON 44

VOCABULARY FOR REVIEW

initiation   rite

SUPPLEMENTARY ACTIVITY

Read James Thurber's short story "The Secret Life of Walter Mitty." In a paragraph or two, show how the story is related to the comments on dreams in the lesson and in mythology in general.

ANSWER KEY

1–10. Answers will vary.
11. The human-animal combinations represent the spiritual vs. the physical, soul vs. body, human vs. beast, noble emotions vs. carnal desires.
12. Represents the courage and strength of the lion and the vigilance and swiftness of the eagle; the eagle represents the divine, and the lion, the human

PRONUNCIATION GUIDE

LESSON 1
Ceres	*Seer eez*
Daedalus	*Ded ul us*
Demeter	*Dih meet ur*
Eurydice	*Yuh rid uh see*
Hades	*Hay deez*
Icarus	*Ik uh rus*
Orpheus	*Or fee us*
Persephone	*Pur sef uh nee*
Pluto	*Plew toe*
Zeus	*Zoos*

LESSON 2
Achilles	*Uh kill eez*
Aphrodite	*Af ruh die tee*
Arachne	*Uh rack nee*
Ares	*Air eez*
Athena	*Uh thee nah*
Cronus	*Kroh nus*
Hermes	*Her meez*
Nike	*Nigh kee*
Styx	*Stiks*

LESSON 3
Hercules	*Her kew leez*
Odysseus	*O dis ee us*

LESSON 4
Cyclops	*Sy clops*
Galatea	*Gal uh tee uh*
Pygmalion	*Pig may lee un*

LESSON 5
Eros	*Ehr ohs*
Hera	*Hee ra*
Mentor	*Men tore*
Midas	*My dus*
Pegasus	*Peg uh sus*
Poseidon	*Poh side un*

LESSON 6
Atropos	*A truh pohs*
Daphne	*Daf nee*
Gaea	*Jee ah*
Iliad	*Ill ee ed*
Janus	*Jay nus*
Jupiter	*Joo pit ur*
Odyssey	*Odd ess ee*
Pandora	*Pan doh ra*
Thetis	*Thee tis*
Titan	*Tite un*
Uranus	*Yoor uh nus*
Woden	*Woe den*

LESSON 7
Chaos	*Kay os*
Cyclops	*Sy klops*
Erebus	*Ehr uh bus*
Nyx	*Niks*

LESSON 8
Epimetheus	*Ep ih mee thee us*
Hestia	*Hes tee ah*
Prometheus	*Proh mee thee us*
Rhea	*Ree uh*

LESSON 9
Cerberus	*Sir bu rus*
Polyphemos	*Pol ah fee mos*

LESSON 10
Argus	*Ar gus*
Artemis	*Art uh mis*
Hephaestus	*Heh fes tus*

LESSON 11
Apollo	*Uh pol oh*
Deimos	*Dee mohs*
Dionysus	*Die uh nee sus*
Eris	*Eh ris*
Phobos	*foh bohs*
Semele	*Sem uh lee*

© 1984, 1997 J. Weston Walch, Publisher

Mythology: A Teaching Unit

Pronunciation Guide (continued)

Lesson 13

Europa	*Yuh **roh** puh*

Lesson 14

Deucalion	*Dyou **kayl** ion*
Penelope	*Pen **ell** oh pee*
Pyrrha	***Pir** uh*
Telemachus	*Tuh **lem** ah kus*

Lesson 15

Bellepheron	*Bu **ler** uh fon*
Helios	***Heel** ee os*
Narcissus	*Nar **sis** us*
Pegasus	***Peg** ah sus*
Phaeton	***Fay** uh ton*

Lesson 16

Acheron	***Ak** uh ron*
Charon	***Kar** un*
Cocytus	*Koh **sy** tus*
Elysian	*Ih **leezh** un*
Ixion	*Ik **see** un*
Lethe	***Lee** thee*
Phlegethon	***Flej** uh thon*
Sisyphus	***Sis** uh fus*
Tantalus	***Tant** uhl us*
Tartarus	***Tart** uh rus*

Lesson 17

Aeacus	***Ee** ah kus*
Agamemnon	*Ag uh **mem** non*
Anticleia	*Ant ih **klee** ah*
Minos	***My** nus*
Neoptolemus	*Nee op **tol** ah mus*
Rhadamanthus	*Rad ah **man** thus*
Tiresias	*Tire **ree** see us*

Lesson 18

Alcmene	*Alk **me** nee*
Augeas	*Aw **je** as*
Centaur	***Sen** tore*
Cerynean	*Ser uh **nee** an*
Deianira	*Dee ah **nee** ra*
Heracles	***Her** uh kleez*
Nessus	***Nes** us*

Lesson 19

Acrisius	*Uh **kris** yus*
Andromeda	*An **drom** ah dah*
Ariadne	*Air ee **ad** nee*
Danaë	***Dan** uh ee*
Graiai	***Gray** yee*
Medusa	*Mih **doo** sah*
Minotaur	***Min** oh tore*
Perseus	***Pur** see us*
Polydectes	*Pol uh **dek** teez*
Theseus	***Thee** see us*

Lesson 20

Briseis	*Bree **see** us*
Calypso	*Kuh **lip** so*
Circe	***Sir** see*
Nausicaa	*Naw **seek** ah a*
Patroclus	*Pah **trow** klus*
Priam	***Pry** um*

Lesson 21

Bacchus	***Bak** us*
Proserpina	*Pro **sur** pee nah*
Vesta	***Ves** tah*

LESSON 23

Balder	*Bohl dur*
Darkalfheim	*Dar kalf haym*
Fenrfr	*Fen reer*
Freya	*Frey uh*
Frigga	*Frig ah*
Jutunheim	*Yoht uhn haym*
Loki	*Loh kee*
Ragnarok	*Rag nuh rock*
Tyr	*Tuhr*
Valhalla	*Val hal uh*
Valkyries	*Val kir eez*

LESSON 24

| Yggdrasil | *Ig druh sil* |
| Niflheim | *Neefl haym* |

LESSON 25

| Beowulf | *Bay oh wolf* |
| Hrothgar | *Wroth gar* |

LESSON 27

Anubis	*uh nyou bus*
Isis	*I suhs*
Nephthys	*Nep tuhs*
Osiris	*Oh sy rus*
Taurt	*Towrt*

LESSON 28

| Horus | *Hor us* |

LESSON 29

| Taut | *Towt* |

LESSON 30

| P'an Ku | *Pahn koo* |
| Taoism | *Tau izm* or *Dau izm* |

LESSON 32

| Tai Shan | *Ti shahn* |

LESSON 33

Brahma	*Bra mah*
Siva	*See vah*
Vishnu	*Vish noo*

LESSON 37

| Nkoyo | *ng koy o* |

© 1984, 1997 J. Weston Walch, Publisher

MYTH, THE MUSEUM OF THE MIND

In a museum, you may already have seen a statue of a Greek goddess or a Roman gladiator. If so, you know how people looked long ago and how they imagined their gods looked.

By reading myths, you can also discover what people thought long ago, what they feared and what they hoped for—even which character traits they admired and which ones they disliked.

What kind of people created these myths? First of all, they were imaginative and capable of telling stories that have lasted for thousands of years.

They were observers of the natural world around them, but they were also in awe of it. They invented stories to account for thunderstorms, floods, eclipses, even the changing seasons, because such occurrences, once explained, seemed less frightening.

They were curious about how the world began and how the first human beings were created; they speculated about death and life after death.

They lived by a moral code that required children to obey parents, parents and children to be reverent to the gods, and all people to be generous to one another.

They pictured their gods as looking and acting as they did themselves. Thus, gods quarreled and were jealous or fell in and out of love, but they were also wise and just. Gods could change their outward forms at will, had superhuman strength, and were immortal. In these last three characteristics, they differed from people.

Because ancient people revealed so much about themselves in their myths, reading those myths, like visiting a museum, makes the past come to life.

FINDING THE MESSAGE IN THE MYTH

Although some myths were probably told simply to entertain listeners, most had a more serious purpose.

A. Some were attempts to explain natural phenomena such as floods.

B. Some were religious speculation on human beings' relationship to the gods or on such mysteries as creation, death, and the afterlife.

C. Some examined human behavior, both people's failings and their virtues.

- Read each of the following well-known myths and decide whether it belongs in Group A, B, or C above. Then state what it explains or teaches.

   1. Daedalus and Icarus
   To escape from a prison where he and his son were being held, Daedalus made wings of wax and feathers. In flight, the son, Icarus, ignored his father's warning about flying too close to the sun. The heat of the sun melted the wax, Icarus's wings fell apart, and he plunged to his death.

   This myth belongs in Group _____ or Group_____ . It teaches

   that _____

   _____

   2. Persephone and Pluto (Hades)
   Persephone, the beautiful daughter of Demeter, goddess of agriculture, was kidnapped by Pluto (Hades) and taken to his kingdom, the Underworld. Demeter, angered by Pluto's boldness and grieving for her daughter, forbade the earth to give forth fruit until Zeus, the most powerful god, worked out a compromise. For five months of the year, Persephone would be with her mother and all growing things would flourish, but during the other seven months she would be with Pluto and the world would turn barren and cold.

   This myth belongs in Group_____. It explains _____

   _____

   3. Orpheus and Eurydice
   Soon after the talented musician Orpheus married the beautiful nymph, Eurydice, she was bitten by a snake and died. Orpheus, determined to bring his bride back from the Under-world, went there himself and so charmed Hades with his music that the god agreed to let Eurydice return to life, on one condition. Orpheus must not look back on Eurydice as he was leading her out of Hades's kingdom. Unfortunately, Orpheus stole one glimpse of his bride and she was lost to him forever.

   This myth could be placed in Group _____ or Group_____. It explains or

   teaches that _____

   _____

- Vocabulary from the myths:

   1. Demeter's Roman name was Ceres. What name for a popular breakfast food is

      derived from it? _____

   2. Orpheum is often used as a name for a theater. Can you explain why this is

      appropriate?_____

© 1984, 1997 J. Weston Walch, Publisher
Mythology: A Teaching Unit

PART I   LESSON 2

MYTHS IN OUR MODERN WORLD

Myths? They are just fantastic stories about the long ago. They don't belong in the twentieth century.

Right?

Wrong! Even though you may not be aware of them, myths still play a part in your daily life.

Perhaps you'd like proof.

Let's imagine that when you got up this morning, you washed your face with Dove soap before going down to breakfast.

While you were eating your cereal, you happened to notice a picture of the corn goddess on the box. Just then, your mother called to you to hurry. You were already late for school, and she'd have to give you a ride in the Mercury.

In your first class, you took out your Venus pencil to do your algebra. English came next. You were expected to write a paragraph, using chronological order. In science, your teacher explained the characteristics of arachnids. In social studies, your class divided into hawks and doves and had a lively debate about our country's military policies.

After school, you put on your Nike running shoes, hoping they'd "put wings on your feet." Later, your track coach told you that your time was off. You thought that was probably because your Achilles tendon was still sore.

Back home, you checked the bulletin board and found that your household chore for the day was cleaning the bathroom with Ajax cleanser.

Finally, with chores and homework finished, you could turn on your Panasonic TV.

How alert were you to the part mythic characters played in your day? Try the game on the next page to find out.

Name _____ Date _____

MYTHIC REFERENCES IN EVERYDAY LIFE

- In the imaginary account of your day, try to find twelve references to myths and list them below. *Clue:* Actually, there are fifteen references. Many are proper nouns or adjectives, but some are indirect references to the characters in the myths.

	MYTHOLOGICAL REFERENCE	DESCRIPTION		MYTHOLOGICAL REFERENCE	DESCRIPTION
1	Dove soap	A	7		
2			8		
3			9		
4			10		
5			11		
6			12		

- Now match the descriptions below with the words or phrases you have written above. For example, "A" is matched with Dove soap because Dove is a *beauty soap* with a *gentle* cleansing action, and because the *dove* was Venus' symbol. *Caution:* A description may be used more than once.

A. Aphrodite (Roman name: Venus) was the goddess of love, beauty, unity, and peace. The gentle dove was her symbol.

B. Ares (Roman name: Mars) was the god of war. Armor, the spear, the dog, and birds of prey were his symbols.

C. Demeter (Roman name: Ceres) was the goddess of agriculture. A popular type of breakfast food derives its name from her Roman name.

D. In American Indian belief, this beautiful goddess was sent by the Great Spirit to teach people how to grow the grain that became an important part of their diet.

E. When this great Greek warrior was a boy, his mother sought to make him immortal by dipping him in the River Styx. But she held him by his heel, and thus that part of him remained forever vulnerable to injury.

F. Like the warrior in Description E, this Greek was capable of destroying all who came his way. Today, a cleanser bears his name.

G. One of the old gods, Cronus, was the father of Zeus. You probably know him as Father Time, the old man with the sickle. In Greek, his name means "time."

H. The goddess Athena taught the young woman Arachne to weave. Arachne became so skillful that she challenged Athena to a weaving contest and so angered the goddess that Athena changed the girl into a spider. Ever since, all spiders are named for Arachne.

I. Hermes (Roman name: Mercury) moved swiftly because he had winged sandals and a winged cap.

J. Nike, the goddess of victory, rewarded the winners of athletic contests. A famous statue of Nike, found on the island of Samothrace, is called the *Winged Victory of Samothrace*.

K. The name of Pan, the god of woods and fields, means "all" or "every." From reeds, Pan made himself a pipe on which he played sad songs in memory of the love he lost.

© 1984, 1997 J. Weston Walch, Publisher   4   *Mythology: A Teaching Unit*

WHERE DO ALL OUR HEROES COME FROM?

Who is the hero of your school? an outstanding athlete? the outspoken editor of your school newspaper? or an ordinary student whose quick thinking saved someone in danger?

Who are our national heroes? sports idols? movie stars? astronauts? or scientists trying to conquer disease?

In other words, what qualities make a hero? Physical strength is one, certainly, as is the will to win, and both are characteristic of great athletes. If we add courage and intelligence, we can see why the crusading editor or the astronaut would also qualify.

But what about the person who risks his life to save another's, or the scientist who devotes a lifetime to relieving pain and suffering? We say such people are altruistic, that is, more interested in others' welfare than in their own. Perhaps that makes them the greatest heroes of all.

In mythology, we shall study ancient heroes such as Achilles, the great warrior; Hercules, the strong man; and Odysseus, the crafty man who was "never at a loss."

From their deeds, we can figure out what ancient people expected of their heroes. They had to be as brave as Achilles, have the superhuman strength of Hercules, and match the cleverness and persistence of Odysseus. A hero had to be a good leader, a father to his followers, merciful to the weak, and merciless to his enemies.

The mercilessness and craftiness that Odysseus showed are not necessarily qualities that we admire today. Yet in books, movies, and TV programs, we like to see the hero triumph over the bad guys, by whatever means.

Of course, the mythical heroes often received help from the gods. The goddess Athena was at Odysseus's side to help him defeat his enemies. With her assistance, Odysseus became superhuman.

Mythical heroes are never real. They simply represent what people at a given time in history saw as the ideal. We have inherited those myths, handed down through the centuries.

Real-life heroes can never become myths, but they can become legends, as more and more stories are told about their lives and deeds. Thus, Martin Luther King, the great crusader for civil rights, has already become a legend; Babe Ruth is legendary in baseball; John Wayne, who always played the good guy in westerns, is a legendary movie star, and Davy Crockett is a legendary frontiersman. No doubt, many other such heroes will appear in your lifetime.

✎ TRACING OUR BELIEFS AND IDEALS TO THEIR SOURCE

In ancient Greece and Rome, warriors were the heroes, because combat—whether to gain territory or take revenge—was a part of everyday life.

In the medieval period, heroes were still fighters, but ideas about the hero, or ideal man, were changing. At King Arthur's court, as you may have read, knights were pledged to use their strength only for good causes. They fought only to help those who were too weak to defend themselves against evil forces. The perfect knight of Arthurian legend was gentler, politer, and more altruistic than the Greek ideal.

Our country has produced its own ideal types. For instance, we admire the self-made person—someone, perhaps from a family with very little money, who has achieved success through his or her own efforts. We admire persistence and the determination to win out over great odds.

Let's look at some American heroes and heroines and think about how they combine the ideal qualities of different periods in history.

1. Abe Lincoln, "the rail-splitter," rose to become president. He is often referred to as the man who freed the slaves. Lincoln is a hero in the minds of Americans because

   _____

   _____

   Clue: What does the description "the rail-splitter" say about his background?

2. Clara Barton almost single-handedly organized the nursing of wounded northern soldiers during the Civil War. She gave up her job, faced many physical hardships, and overcame much opposition to her work. What heroic qualities does this information about Barton bring to mind? _____

   _____

3. John F. Kennedy's administration as president is often described as "Camelot," the name of King Arthur's court. What does "Camelot" say about Kennedy's ideals? How does that name help to make him seem more heroic?

   _____

   Clue: Remember King Arthur's aims and remember that he is always described as a hero in our literature.

4. Sojourner Truth, an escaped slave with no education, became an effective speaker and campaigner for the cause of abolition (freedom for the slaves). What heroic qualities did

   Truth display? _____

   _____

   How did she resemble Lincoln? _____

5. Many of our contemporary heroes are in the world of sports. How are their accomplish-

   ments similar to those of ancient heroes? _____

   Clue: Is a game a kind of combat? Is gain or loss of territory involved?

WHY STUDY MYTHS? 1

Perhaps you have seen the movie *Excalibur* or a rerun of *Camelot*. Both are versions of the King Arthur legend, a story that has been told and retold throughout the centuries. The musical the comedy *My Fair Lady*, was based on a play by modern playwright George Bernard Shaw, who based his play on the ancient Greek myth of Pygmalion and Galatea.

Myths have always provided inspiration for writers, artists, and composers. That's why knowing the myths can help you to appreciate art and music and to understand literature.

You gain other advantages from knowing the myths—you are able to recognize and understand allusions (references) to them, which writers often use to make a point. Of course, *allusion* is a general term; not all the allusions that writers make are to myths. But we'll get to that in a minute. Allusions may be new to you, but probably you have already encountered metaphors and similes and know that both are comparisons. The difference between them is that a simile states the comparison clearly, using *like* or *as*, while a metaphor only suggests it..

Simile: *"I'm as restless as a willow in a windstorm."*

Metaphor: *He pussyfooted up the stairs.*

The metaphor does not state, but merely suggests, that the person's movements are as stealthy and quiet as a cat's.

Now for the allusion. Suppose a friend tells you that he has nicknamed the new teacher Ichabod Crane. He's using an allusion, but you won't know its significance unless you have read "The Legend of Sleepy Hollow," by Washington Irving. In that short story, the schoolmaster, Ichabod Crane, is tall, thin, and awkward looking.

If, when you have slept late on Saturday morning, your father greets you with "Here comes Rip Van Winkle," you won't be sure what he means unless you understand his reference or allusion. Rip Van Winkle, another Washington Irving character, slept for twenty years!

Do you see that allusions can be a kind of comparison? Now let's find out what you can do with some mythological allusions.

Name _____ Date _____

 # LEARNING TO READ THE LANGUAGE OF ALLUSION

Helen, thy beauty is to me
Like those Nicean barks of yore,
That gently, o'er a perfumed sea,
The weary, wayworn wanderer bore
To his own native shore.
—from Edgar Allan Poe's "To Helen"

(Nicean = Greek; bark = sailing ship)

Poe wrote this poem for a real woman; she was not named Helen. He uses allusion to suggest that she is like Helen of Troy, the most beautiful woman in the ancient world. When Helen was stolen from her husband by a Trojan prince, the Greeks went to war against Troy. Returning from the war, the Greeks made slow progress toward home, thus the reference to the "weary, wayworn wanderer." Can you see how a knowledge of myth is necessary to make the poem's allusions understandable?

- Now it's your turn. See if you can recognize the mythical source of the allusions that follow.

    A. *Hark! Hark! the lark at heaven's gate sings*
       And Phoebus' gins to rise
       His steeds to water at those springs
       On chalic'd flowers that lie
       —from William Shakespeare's *Cymbeline*

('gins is a contraction of begins,
chalic'd is another contraction
and means cuplike; steeds are horses.)

1. What was Phoebus's Greek name? _____

2. The myth alluded to concerns the Greeks' belief that _____, the sun god, drove his chariot across the _____ . It was their way of accounting for the sun's journey from sunrise to sunset.

3. What or where is "heaven's gate"?

   _____

4. In the poem, what time of day is it?

   _____

5. Can you name a chaliced, or cuplike, flower?

   _____

    B. *He who died*
       For soaring too audacious near the sun
       Where that same treacherous wax began to run.
          —from John Keats's "Endymion"

(audacious = daring)

✏️ LEARNING TO READ THE LANGUAGE OF ALLUSION (CONTINUED)

6. This poem refers or alludes to the myth of _____ and _____

7. Who was "too audacious" and what happened to him? _____
_____

   Keats's title "Endymion" is also an allusion. He wrote the poem in tribute to a friend who died while he was still a very young man. In the myths, Endymion was the beloved of Diana (Artemis), but Jupiter (Zeus) interfered and gave the youth a choice between death and perpetual sleep. Endymion chose sleep and thus remained young forever.

   C. *I inclined*
   To lose my faith in Ballyrush and Gortin
   Till Homer's ghost came whispering to my mind,
   He said, "I made the Iliad *from such a local row.*
   Gods make their own importance.
                    —from Patrick Kavanagh's "Epic"

   In this poem, the Irish poet Patrick Kavanagh describes how his neighbors in two little villages of Country Monaghan fight fiercely over bits s of stony land. The time is just before World War II, and at first Kavanagh thinks that with Europe on the brink of war, such arguments are insignificant.

8. Who was Homer? _____
_____
_____

9. What was the *Iliad* about? _____
_____
_____

10. In your words, what advice does Homer give Kavanagh? _____
_____
_____
_____
_____
_____
_____
_____
_____
_____
_____

 # WHY STUDY MYTHS? II

When you were in elementary school, your teacher may have pasted gold stars on your best papers. For a special February holiday, the teachers probably decorated the windows and bulletin boards with red cardboard cupids and hearts. Of course, in every classroom, an American flag hung.

The gold stars, the cardboard cupids, even the flag are all symbols. That is, they represent something beyond themselves: the stars represent achievement; the cupids, Valentine's Day; and the flag, our country.

By now you are becoming aware of the part myths play in our daily lives and will not be surprised that many familiar symbols have their origin in mythology. Take that Valentine's Day cupid, for example. In Roman mythology, Cupid (Greek name: Eros) was the son of Venus, goddess of love. Any victim of Cupid's arrows was supposed to fall in love immediately. Appropriately, Cupid is the symbol of our most romantic holiday.

Do you know why the owl symbolizes wisdom and the peacock, pride? The owl was associated with Athena, goddess of wisdom, while the peacock was favored by Hera, wife of Zeus, a proud and vain goddess.

Zeus, the most powerful of the gods, had a favorite bird, too, the eagle, king of the birds. Thus, our American eagle, which appears on the Great Seal of the United States, can be said to represent freedom and power.

Other mythological symbols are all around you. As you grow more familiar with the stories of the Greek gods and heroes, you will find yourself becoming aware of the role myth plays in advertisements.

Name _____ Date _____

 # RECOGNIZING SYMBOLS FROM THE MYTHS

- Ten familiar advertising symbols are listed below in Column A. Try matching them with the appropriate mythological figures in Column B. One figure in Column B is used twice.

COLUMN A

A. the Florists' Transworld Delivery (FTD) symbol of a male figure with wings on his cap and sandals

B. the medical profession's symbol of a winged sword or wand with two snakes twined around it

C. Mobil Oil Corporation's symbol of a flying red horse

D. Midas Muffler Shops' gold-painted mufflers

E. the owl, emblem of the publishers Henry Holt & Co.

F. Goodyear Tire's symbol of a winged sandal

G. figure of a man playing pipes, emblem of Pan Books Limited

H. Mentor Books as the name of a series of reference books published by New American Library

I. Atlas Van Lines as the name of a moving company

J. Trident Packing Company, the name of a fish-canning company

COLUMN B

_____ Mentor was a wise Greek, friend and adviser to the hero Odysseus.

_____ A god punished King Midas for his greed by causing everything he touched to turn to gold.

_____ Poseidon, god of the sea, carried a trident, or three-pronged spear.

_____ Hermes, swift messenger of the gods, wore a winged cap and winged sandals.

_____ Pegasus, the flying horse of the myths, actually flew up into the heavens.

_____ The owl, bird of Athena, goddess of wisdom, represented silence, meditation, and wisdom.

_____ Hermes tested the power of his wand by placing it between two fighting serpents. They immediately stopped fighting. The wand came to represent peace and healing.

_____ Pan, the woodland god, is often pictured playing his pipes.

_____ Atlas, a strong giant, supported the heavens on his shoulders.

- Matching the symbols with the descriptions was probably easy for you. In a class discussion, could you explain why each symbol is appropriate for the company that uses it?

 **WHY STUDY MYTHS III**

If someone told you there was a fast way to increase your vocabulary without having to memorize word lists, wouldn't you be eager to know the details?

It's no secret. Studying mythology gives you a key that unlocks the meanings of many words. You won't find those meanings hard to remember if you associate them with the myths from which they are derived.

Very often, adjectives are formed from a mythological character's name.

Example: *halcyon* from Halcyone.

> Halcyon means "calm,
> peaceful, tranquil."

In the myth, Halcyone was turned into a kingfisher by the goddess Thetis. The Greeks believed that this bird's nesting period was at the winter solstice and that the kingfisher raised its young in nests floating on the sea. Observing that a period of calm weather usually occurred at this time, they believed that Thetis calmed the sea for the birds' benefit. Thus, today we say that halcyon days are calm and peaceful days.

Sometimes a mythological name is retained as a common noun.

Example: *mentor* from Mentor.

> Mentor means "a wise and
> loyal adviser."

In the Greek poet Homer's epic poems, *The Iliad* and *The Odyssey*, Mentor is a wise old man who gives advice to other Greeks.

Occasionally, verbs come from the myths.

Example: *atrophy* from Atropos.

> Atrophy means "to waste or
> wither away."

Atropos was the name of one of the three Fates. It was her job to cut the thread of life, thus ending a human existence.

Names with mythological derivations appear in geography (Europe from Europa); the calendar (Wednesday or Woden's Day); astronomy (Uranus, Pluto); botany (narcissus); zoology (arachnids); and anatomy (the Achilles tendon).

Certain phrases we use have also been borrowed from the myths. Thus, "to have the Midas touch" is to have the knack of making money. "To open a Pandora's box" is to bring troubles upon oneself, and "to sow dragon's teeth" is to behave in such a way as to stir up argument or war. Even weapons like the Nike and Titan missiles take their names from mythological characters.

Do you see that those phrases, which have become synonyms for certain types of behavior, are also allusions? You'll learn more about the stories they come from later.

Now let's find out how many words from the myths you have already acquired.

Name _____ Date _____

 # WORDS FROM THE GODS

panic	atlas	cereal	erotic	syringe
plutonium	herculean	cloth	pantheist	Orpheum
martial	phobia	geography	arachnids	lethal
chronological	Junoesque	odyssey	atrophy	pandemonium
Jovian	mercurial			

• Match each definition with a word from the list above. You may need the dictionary.

1. _____ a book of maps, named for the mythical character who held up the heavens

2. _____ arranged in order of occurrence, from Zeus's father, whose name meant time

3. _____ the study of the continents, climates, plants, animals, etc., named for Gaea (pronounced *Jee ah*)or earth

4. _____ warlike, derived from the name of the Roman god of war

5. _____ a wasting away or failure to grow, from Atropos, the Fate who decided how long each person's life should be

6. _____ a kind of breakfast food, from the name of the Roman goddess of the harvest; also any kind of grain, such as wheat or rye

7. _____ spiders, named for the maiden who challenged Athena to a weaving contest

8. _____ an irrational and persistent fear, named for the god of fear

9. _____ a sudden fear, named for the god of fields and woods, Who sometimes caused groundless fear among mortals.

10. _____ a scene of wild disorder, noise, and confusion, name of the god in 9

11. _____ a believer that god is everywhere, in everything, and that everything is good, named for the god in 9

12. _____ a tube with a rubber bulb that draws and ejects liquid, named for the beloved of Pan, who was turned into a hollow reed

13. _____ a radioactive chemical element named for the god of the Underworld

14. _____ fatal, deadly, suggestive of death, from the river of forgetfulness in Hades

15. _____ a term for fabrics, from the Fate who spun life's thread

16. _____ having to do with sexual love, taken from the Greek name of Cupid

17. _____ an extended journey, from the name of a hero who wandered for many years

18. _____ adjective meaning "stately and queenlike," from the queen of the Roman gods

19. _____ difficult, requiring great strength or courage, from a mythical Greek strongman

20. _____ quick-witted, changeable, fickle, as was the messenger of the gods

21. _____ majestic, from the name of the Roman king of the gods

22. _____ name given to a music hall or theater, from the musician whose playing charmed Hades

PART I LESSON 7

LET'S TAKE A LOOK AT HOW IT ALL BEGAN

You may remember from Lesson 1 that many myths were created because of people's need to explain natural phenomena, such as thunderstorms, the changing seasons, even night and day. We could say that people needed to be reassured that those events followed some pattern.

Of even greater importance was the need for some explanation of how the world began and how its people came to exist. Therefore, all ancient societies developed a creation myth. For example, the American Indians imagined that their world had been created by an animal. This was a natural assumption since they lived closely with the animals and depended on animals for their very existence.

The Greeks had a different explanation. They believed that Chaos was the first state of the universe. As you might guess from the word chaos, no order existed, and there was no light.

From this nothingness arose Nyx (night) and Erebus (the personification of darkness). Next came Eros, which represented both love and the principle of order. (In later myths, Eros became the god of love.)

Finally, Eros achieved harmony (order) by bringing together Gaea, or Earth (the female force), and Uranus, or Sky (the male Force). From their union came three hundred-handed monsters, three one-eyed giants, and the Titans.

Gaea is also credited with producing the mountains and seas, but it is her Titan children who are of special interest to us because although they were giants, they were human in form. Thus, the Greeks had begun to imagine their gods to be like themselves in appearance.

Cronus was the youngest of these Titans. He was destined to cause his father's fall from power.

Uranus, Cronus's father, was terrified of his giant children and fearful that they would overthrow him. To prevent that, he had been burying them alive. Gaea, their mother, was powerless to stop him. Finally, she persuaded Cronus to take revenge for his brothers and sisters. In anger, Cronus took a sickle, mutilated his father, and then seized the position of supreme ruler.

Certainly, Uranus seems to have been an unnatural father and Cronus an unnatural son, but actually their behavior is symbolic, not only of the Greek way of life, but also perhaps of our own. Eventually, don't the children (the new generation) replace the parents? Haven't we seen old governments overthrown or replaced by a new one? Even in business, aren't the older executives or leaders forced to move out to make way for "young blood"?

Perhaps the Greek account isn't as fanciful as it first appears.

✎ WORDS AND MEANINGS
FROM THE CREATION MYTH

- First, let's try a vocabulary review. List at least eight nouns, adjectives, or adverbs derived from the names in today's lesson. You may need to consult a dictionary.

NAMES	WORDS DERIVED FROM THEM
1. **Cronus**	_____
2. **Gaea**	_____
3. **Eros**	_____
4. **Chaos**	_____

5. People who achieve great success in business or industry are sometimes described as titans. The most modern ship of its time and one of the largest was the *Titanic*. We have produced the Titan missile. In each of these examples, why is the use of *titan* or *titanic* appropriate?

_____

_____

_____

_____

6. Even today, we use expressions such as "Mother Earth" or "Mother Nature." Explain briefly where these names probably came from.

_____

_____

_____

_____

7. In today's myth, Uranus feared his children and saw them as a threat to his power. Is the mythmaker suggesting anything about the ancient Greeks' government? For example, do you think it was stable? Explain.

_____

_____

_____

_____

THE GODS GIVE WAY TO THE NEW

In Lesson 7, you learned the Greek version of the creation of the world. Now you may be wondering when human beings entered the picture. Actually, that did not take place until after another power struggle among the gods.

It happened like this. Cronus was now in power, but just like his father before him, he saw everyone else as a threat to his throne. As a result, he decided to leave the three hundred-handed monsters and the one-eyed giants buried. He released only his fellow Titans.

He was suspicious of his own children, too, but instead of burying them alive as Uranus had done, he ate them! Cronus's wife, Rhea, tolerated his behavior for a while. Then, like Gaea, she plotted against her husband. Just after Rhea had given birth to a son, Zeus, she arranged for him to be taken to a distant place where he would be safe from his father. Then she wrapped a large stone in a cloth, and the unsuspecting Cronus ate it, thinking that he was destroying his latest son.

When Zeus had grown to manhood, he returned home unrecognized. Then he found a way to feed Cronus an herb which caused him to vomit violently, thus releasing the eleven children he had swallowed long before.

Zeus now had eleven allies, and he also enlisted the help of two sympathetic Titans, Prometheus and Epimetheus. Next, he released the one-eyed giants, or Cyclopes, who had been buried all this time, knowing that they too would have a grudge against Cronus. Even with all those allies, Zeus found his father to be a formidable opponent. Their power struggle lasted ten long years, but finally Cronus was deposed and Zeus became the supreme ruler.

Like many real-life conquering heroes, Zeus rewarded his followers in various ways, but he divided his father's kingdom with his two brothers. Poseidon was to be god of the sea; and Hades, god of the Underworld. Naturally, Zeus kept the best for himself and became god of the sky and the upper world.

If we read the myth of Rhea's deception of Cronus literally, it is simply a fantastic story; but if we see it as symbolic, it begins to make sense. Certainly, we can accept that Cronus was deposed through his wife's trickery and his grown son's rebellion. History has parallels to support such acts. For example, the twelfth-century English King Henry II was the victim of various plots hatched by his jealous sons with the aid of their mother, Queen Eleanor of Aquitaine.

At any rate, Zeus's coming to power set the stage for the arrival of human beings, whom he needed to worship him. But before you find out how humans came on the scene, you should become a little better acquainted with the gods themselves.

THE GODS' FAMILY TREE.

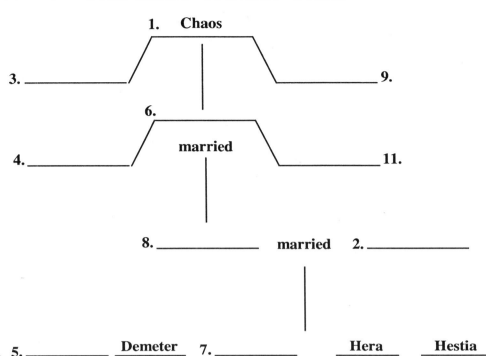

- You may have seen a family tree showing your relationship to your living relatives and your ancestors. Today, you are going to create a family tree for the gods. First, fill in the space beside each description with the name of the appropriate god or goddess; you may have to refer to earlier lessons. Then write the name in the corresponding blank on the tree (the first one is done for you). Note that the goddesses Hera, Hestia, and Demeter already appear on the tree. You will learn more about them later

1. __Chaos_____ This was the beginning; no order existed; all was darkness.
2. _____ She fed her husband a stone wrapped like an infant.
3. _____ This figure personified the night.
4. _____ He buried his children alive.
5. _____ He became the god of the Underworld.
6. _____ The principle of love and order, it arose from night and darkness.
7. _____ He became the supreme god, ruler of heaven and earth.
8. _____ He mutilated his father with a sickle.
9. _____ This figure was a personification of darkness.
10. _____ Zeus made him god of the sea.
11. _____ She plotted with her youngest son to overthrow her husband.

ZEUS AND HIS BROTHERS

From your introduction to him in Lesson 8, you know that Zeus was clever. Remember how he fed his unsuspecting father an herb so that Cronus would disgorge his children? Zeus was also aggressive and ambitious, a fighter who did not hesitate to depose his father and take over the throne. And he was also cruel and relentless, as you will see when you read about his treatment of the Titan Prometheus, who had been his ally.

But, for the Greeks, Zeus was the supreme god. We can assume that these qualities he displayed were ones they saw as necessary in a leader.

Zeus was also a father figure. The Greeks believed that he determined how human beings should behave and punished wrongdoers. They feared his wrath and the thunderbolts he could hurl from the sky.

But Zeus had human failings, too. He was often unfaithful to his wife and had love affairs with mortal maidens. Here is evidence that the Greeks endowed their gods with both the good and bad traits they themselves possessed.

Zeus's brother Poseidon was also a powerful and wrathful god, restless as the sea, which was his home. To the Greeks, whose land was nearly surrounded by water, he was important because in his good moods he protected navigation and commerce. In his bad moods, however, he caused storms and earthquakes. Like Zeus, he was relentless toward those who offended him—as the hero Odysseus discovered. Having blinded Poseidon's one-eyed son, Polyphemos, Odysseus was doomed to roam the seas for ten years before he was allowed to return to his home on the island of Ithaca.

The third brother, Hades, guardian of the Underworld, was a shadowy figure. Black-cloaked and gloomy, he seemed as mysterious as the infernal regions where he dwelt and whose gates were guarded by the many-headed dog, Cerberus. But the Greeks believed that he protected the harvests, and they knew that his kingdom yielded great riches in minerals and metals.

Hades acted merely as the custodian of the dead; it was not his role to decide the fate of those who came into his domain. Three judges did that. Yet he was so feared that his name was seldom mentioned. Since he offered no threat of punishment and he almost never left the Underworld, the fear of him was just a reflection of the fear of death. For the Greeks, the afterlife offered little reward, even for those whose life on earth had been exemplary.

Name _____   Date _____

 # SYMBOLIC LANGUAGE FROM THE GODS

The Greeks imagined Zeus and Poseidon as powerfully built, bearded gods. Zeus held thunderbolts in one hand while Poseidon grasped a three-pronged spear, or trident. Zeus was depicted as bare to the waist, and Poseidon wore little or no clothing; but Hades was shown fully clothed, seated at a table, with a scepter in his hand. The animals, plants, and symbols associated with each god are listed below.

Zeus	Animals:	eagle and ox
	Plant:	oak tree
	Symbols:	scepter, throne, thunderbolt, double-bladed ax
Poseidon	Animals:	dolphin
	Plant:	ash tree, pine tree, water plants
	Symbols:	anchor, chariot, shell, ship's tiller or prow, trident
Hades	Animals:	many-headed dog named Cerberus, black sheep
	Plant:	poppy, cypress tree
	Symbols:	scepter, throne, cornucopia, the color black

• Following are a number of words and expressions in our language that still have some association with the Greeks' beliefs about the gods. Match each word or expression with the correct definition.

WORD OR EXPRESSION   DEFINITION

A. **poppy**   _____ one who guards people or places

B. **eagle-eyed**   _____ despondency, melancholy

C. **watchdog**   _____ a sleep-inducing plant

D. **underworld**   _____ the color of mourning

E. **undercover agent**   _____ describing a keen observer

F. **black sheep**   _____ the world of organized crime

G. **thunderstruck**   _____ one who does not live up to his family's expectations and reputation

H. **oak tree**   _____ awed, bowled over

I. **cornucopia**   _____ instrument used to keep a ship on course

J. **tiller**   _____ horn of plenty

K. **black**   _____ tree known for sturdiness

L. **cypress**   _____ friendly animal reputed to help seamen

M. **ox**   _____ tree often planted in cemeteries

N. **shady deal**   _____ a questionable business transaction

O. **black mood**   _____ one who tries to discover secrets

P. **dolphin**   _____ an animal with great physical strength

© 1984, 1997 J. Weston Walch, Publisher   *Mythology: A Teaching Unit*

THE MAJOR GODDESSES

Hera, one of Zeus's three sisters, became his wife. She was the queen of the heavens and the goddess of marriage and childbirth. The Greeks imagined her as a nagging wife—beautiful, but vain and vindictive. They told many stories of her cruelty to any girl who happened to arouse her husband's interest.

The peacock was Hera's favorite bird. The design on its tail feathers represented the hundred eyes of Argus, which Hera had transplanted there to help her keep watch over Zeus.

Demeter was also a sister of Zeus. You may remember the story of Hades's kidnapping of her daughter Persephone. It was said that as Demeter roamed the earth mourning for her daughter, she lit two torches and with them set fire to Mount Etna. Its volcano is still active today.

Demeter was also a goddess of marriage; but she is best known as the goddess of the harvest, who introduced agriculture to the Greeks. To offend her was to bring blight and drought to the crops and famine to themselves, the people believed; so they held frequent festivals in her honor.

The third sister, Hestia, was not given the prominence of the other two. She was the goddess of the hearth fire and a protectress of the household and the people themselves.

Aphrodite, the goddess of love and beauty, was even lovelier than Hera, which did not endear her to that vain immortal. Ironically, Aphrodite was married to the physically unattractive

Hephaestus, blacksmith to the gods. Like Zeus, who in some myths is said to be her father, she was unfaithful in marriage and had many love affairs. It is clear that the Greeks considered her basically immoral; but despite that weakness in her character, they admired her beauty and believed she personified peace, unity, and order. Appropriately, the white dove is her symbol.

Aphrodite is supposed to have been born from the foam of the sea, but the goddess Athena had an even more unusual birth. She is supposed to have sprung to life from Zeus's forehead, fully grown, completely clothed, and armed for battle.

The child of Zeus's brain, Athena became the goddess of wisdom, with the owl as her symbol. In some myths, she is credited with helping Prometheus bring the sacred fire to man. (We'll get to that story in Lesson 12.) At any rate, she was much admired by the Greeks, who named Athens after her and built the Parthenon in her honor.

Artemis, also a daughter of Zeus, was the moon goddess. The Greeks imagined her as a young and beautiful huntress, changeable in form and nature. She was sometimes friendly, protecting virgins and travelers. She was a patroness of marriage and a helper in childbirth. But she could cause sudden death, shooting unlucky females with her arrows, and she was believed to cause madness. Truly, she was an unpredictable goddess.

Name _____ Date _____

 # HOW WELL DO YOU KNOW THE GODDESSES?

- You may need a dictionary to check the meanings of the following words.

    A. **moonstruck**   meaning: _____

    B. **brainchild**   meaning: _____

    C. **aphrodisiac**   meaning: _____

- From your knowledge of the goddesses, state which one could be connected with each of the above words and give a reason for your choice.

    A. _____

    B. _____

    C. _____

- A newspaper, no longer published, was called *The Eastern Argus*. Why was that an appropriate name for a newspaper?

    D. _____

    What do you think is the origin of our expression "proud as a peacock"?

    E. _____

- Imagine that a newspaper was published on Mount Olympus, where the gods lived, and that Olympia's advice column appeared in it. Which goddess might have written each of the following letters?

    Dear Olympia,

    I am an attractive woman of an "interesting age." My friends tell me that I am as beautiful as ever, but my husband is no longer attentive to me. Nothing I say has any influence on him, although I say quite a bit. He continues to stay out late. I am certain he is seeing other women. What can I do to win him back?

    Signed: *Anxious*

    F. Which goddess wrote it? _____

    Dear Olympia,

    I have been a faithful reader of your column for years and hope that you can help me as you have helped others. You see, all my life people have been telling me that I am a great beauty. I admit that men have always found me attractive, and I used to have a wonderful time at parties. I married recently, and my husband is a good man and hardworking, although he is not much to look at. The trouble is that he's away a great deal, working at his forge, and I do get lonely. Do you think it would be wrong for me to go out for an occasional social evening?

    Signed: *Doubtful*

    G. Who wrote the letter? _____

OTHER GREAT OLYMPIANS

Apollo, the sun god, was especially important to farmers, but important to seagoing Greeks, too, because he guided navigators. He had many powers: as a healer of the sick and protector of crops, as a shepherd, as a musician, and as the patron of oratory, art, poetry, and science. The Greeks held him in such esteem that they built a temple at Delphi in his honor; its oracle became famous throughout the ancient world. It was believed that Apollo had gone down into darkness and risen again; thus, he became a symbol of resurrection and eternal life. He also represented order, purity, and reasonableness.

Another god, Dionysus, also experienced a kind of death and rebirth. He represented the earth itself as it went through the cycle of fall, winter, and spring. He was best known, though, as the god of the wine, and wine played an important part in the life of the Greeks.

The stories of Dionysus's birth vary, but in one he is the child of Zeus and Semele, one of Zeus's many mortal lovers. In another story, jealous Hera is supposed to have driven him mad. At any rate, wherever Dionysus went, he was followed by frenzied females dressed in animal skins. Their wild and noisy behavior (from which our word orgy comes) caused him to be associated with intoxication. But he was also credited with teaching the Greeks how to cultivate their crops. He was the god of fertility and of inspiration. His festival, held each year in Athens, was actually a literary contest at which many great Greek tragedies and comedies were first performed.

You have already met the god Hephaestus, blacksmith of the gods and husband of Aphrodite. An outcast among the gods because he was lame and ugly, he was a great craftsman who produced armor for the heroes, fashioning it on his anvil located in Mount Etna. The volcano's sparks were said to come from his forge.

One of his rivals for the affection of Aphrodite was Ares, god of war. In the myths, Ares appears as a fickle, bloodthirsty, and bullying character, with no redeeming features. He was the twin brother of Eris (strife). His horses were Deimos (panic) and Phobos (fear). It is a contradiction that although the Greeks revered their military heroes, they disliked the god of war. Evidently, they saw war as an ugly necessity.

The last of the great Olympians is one whose physical form is probably familiar to you. He is Hermes, the well-known symbol of the Florists' Transworld Delivery system. He was the messenger of the gods and represented the wind, which he resembled in his swiftness and his unpredictability. His functions offer an indication of his character. He was the go-between for the living and the dead and escorted souls down to Hades. He was the god of commerce and science and of luck and wealth, but he was also the patron of thieves and vagabonds. He invented the lyre and gave it to his brother Apollo, but only after he had stolen Apollo's oxen. In short, like the Greeks themselves, he had both good and bad traits.

✎ MORE WORDS FROM THE GODS

- First, let's try a little vocabulary study. Write what you think is the definition of each of the next four words. Then use the dictionary to check and correct your definition.

WORD	DEFINITION
orgy	_____
phobia	_____
panic	_____
lyric	_____

- Now use the dictionary to define the next four words. Write their meanings in the space provided.

satyr	_____
acrophobia	_____
claustrophobia	_____
hydrophobia	_____

- Now fill in the blanks in the following sentences with the appropriate words from the two lists above.

1. Because of my tendency to _____ , I was reluctant to go to the top of the Empire State Building.

2. If you are a victim of _____ , you may find it difficult to enter an elevator.

3. Because the people did not show moderation in their drinking, what had begun as a pleasant party soon became an _____ .

4. Many _____ poems have been set to music; an example is "Drink to Me Only with Thine Eyes."

5. When I came face to face with a bear in the woods, I began to _____ .

6. People who have a _____ about germs are constantly washing their hands.

7. _____ is a disease characterized by a strong reluctance to drink water.

8. In paintings, Dionysus is often shown surrounded by _____ .

9. After reading Lesson 11, you may already realize that Apollo and Athena were the most admired Greek god and goddess. What does that indicate to you about what the Greeks considered to be ideal characteristics? _____

_____

The brief accounts in the last three lessons demonstrate the vividness of the Greek imagination and the personal way the Greeks saw their gods. More important, because these accounts show you traits of character the Greeks admired or despised, they enable you to understand the Greeks better. That is important because ancient Greek thought still has a tremendous influence in our modern world.

THE CREATION OF MAN AND WOMAN

Once Zeus had seized power from Cronus and gained dominion over the heavens and earth, he wanted some beings capable of admiring and worshiping him. But Zeus did not choose to create these beings himself. The task went to the slow-witted Titan Epimetheus, who, with his brother Prometheus, had helped Zeus to defeat Cronus.

Epimetheus fashioned all the creatures of the earth from clay. Having given them life, he gave each species a quality that would ensure its survival. Prometheus, meanwhile, made a creature that was godlike in its physical form. But Epimetheus had already doled out all the special powers and nothing was left to give this poor human being as protection against larger, stronger, or faster animals.

At this point, having the foresight that Epimetheus lacked, Prometheus realized that human beings, fashioned in the gods' image, must be given a power that would make them superior to all other animals and truly godlike.

He decided to steal Zeus's sacred fire from Mount Olympus and bring it to mankind in a hollow reed (lightning bolt). Prometheus's gift was a generous one. With that celestial fire, human beings became so powerful that Zeus began to feel threatened and was gravely displeased. Zeus chained the Titan to Mount Caucasus as a punishment. Next, determined to undo the good that Prometheus had done, Zeus commissioned Hephaestus to fashion a creature that would be destined to bring misery to mankind.

That creature was Pandora, the first woman. The gods showered gifts upon her. Athena taught her to weave; Aphrodite gave her great beauty; but Hermes made her deceitful and thieving. Against his brother's advice, Epimetheus then married this radiant creature, thus helping to fulfill Zeus's long-range plan.

Epimetheus was the keeper of a strongbox that was never to be opened; it contained all the blessings intended for human beings. (In another version of the myth, it contained all the evils.) Zeus knew that Pandora's curiosity would drive her to open the box. Of course, she did open it and—depending on which myth you read—either let all our human blessings fly away or let loose all evils upon us. In either myth, only Hope remained in the box—and Zeus had succeeded in bringing misery to mankind.

Nor were Prometheus's troubles over. Like other rulers before him, Zeus feared being overthrown and believed that Prometheus knew when and how this would happen. He promised to free Prometheus in return for his knowledge. When the Titan refused the offer, Zeus sent a vulture to tear out his liver each day. Each night it grew back, so the torture continued for centuries, until Hercules came to Prometheus's rescue.

This creation myth tells us quite a bit about the way the Greeks thought, but we must understand the symbolic language of the story. First of all, it says that human beings do not have the physical strength to compete with the other creatures of the world, but that given the advantage of that divine spark, intellect, they are superior to other animals.

Next, from the Pandora story we can tell that if Epimetheus had not been tempted by Pandora's physical charm, if he had listened to reason and not been swayed by emotion, his life and the lives of human beings would have been serene. As for the beautiful but impulsive and deceitful Pandora, her character shows us that the Greeks did not hold women in high esteem; they saw women as creatures of emotion rather than intellect.

Name _____ Date _____

✎ READING THE MORAL IN THE MYTH

- The Greek story of creation can actually be seen as a series of contests: between Zeus and Prometheus; between Pandora and her husband, who had forbidden her to open the box; between reason and emotion; and even between good and evil. Let's look for a moment at the contest of wills between Zeus and Prometheus. Prometheus represents intellect, selflessness, and devotion to principle. (Prometheus refuses Zeus's offer because he sees Zeus as an unjust ruler.) Zeus, on the other hand, is harsh, vengeful, and jealous of his power—which is physical rather than intellectual. He may be the actual ruler, but he is not the ideal one.

Now you have a chance to take another look at each of these contestants and see how they fared. In the following sentences, fill in the blanks to complete the statement.

1. Prometheus was punished for doing a good deed. But Prometheus did _____ fire to bring it to mankind, and he _____ the supreme ruler, Zeus.

2. Having deposed Cronus, Zeus was the supreme ruler and was able to take revenge on those who offended him. But Zeus did not have Prometheus's power to _____ the future, and Zeus _____ that he might be overthrown.

3. Epimetheus had the honor of creating all the animals, and he married a beautiful woman. But he lacked _____ and did not recognize _____ advice when he heard it.

4. Pandora was beautiful and was favored by the gods. But her _____ and her _____ brought trouble upon her and everyone else.

   The myth seems to point out that whatever our motives and whatever our capabilities, we must expect to take the consequences for our action.

5. There is an obvious parallel to Pandora's act in the Christian belief. What is it?

6. The English poet Alexander Pope once wrote:

   Hope springs eternal in the human breast;
   Man never is, but always to be blessed;

- Paraphrased, Pope is saying that human beings are always hopeful—that they never feel blessed at a given moment, but that they always expect to be. Is Pope's statement related to the myth of Pandora's box? Explain.

_____

_____

_____

_____

PART I

THE GODS AS LOVERS

LESSON 13

The last lesson showed you the gods in some of their most favorable and unfavorable aspects. Prometheus was courageous, selfless, and long-suffering; Zeus, ruthless and cunning; Epimetheus, stupid and thoughtless; and Pandora, untrustworthy. In other words, the Greeks endowed the gods with the good and bad traits they saw in each other.

Today's stories of Zeus, Apollo, and Artemis reveal each of them as a god or goddess with very human desires.

Let's look first at the myth of Zeus and Europa, a Phoenician princess. Like Persephone, who was kidnapped by Hades while she was in a field picking flowers, Europa had been playing in a field with other young girls when she was kidnapped by Zeus. To lure her away, he assumed the form of a gentle white bull, and the other girls amused themselves by hanging garlands around his neck. But Zeus soon persuaded Europa to climb onto his back, and when she did, he carried her away to a land he called Europa (Europe) in her honor. Zeus fathered Europa's three sons, who eventually became the judges in Hades.

Apollo, too, was susceptible to the charms of mortal maidens, but he was not always as successful as Zeus in his love affairs. When Apollo became infatuated with Cassandra, daughter of King Priam of Troy, she promised to marry him if he gave her the gift of prophecy. Apollo kept his part of the bargain, but Cassandra refused to marry him. This was Apollo's revenge: He said

that Cassandra would keep the gift of prophecy, but that no one would ever believe her predictions. Thus, she would never be successful in warning people of dangers ahead. Her gift would only bring her frustration.

Apollo also fell in love with Daphne, the daughter of a river god. But Daphne did not return his affection. In fact, she fled from him. Apollo pursued her, but when she was almost within his grasp, Daphne called upon the gods to save her. Astonished, Apollo saw the beautiful nymph turn into a laurel tree before his very eyes. Because he had loved her so much, Apollo said that, in her memory, the laurel would always be sacred to him.

Apollo's sister, the goddess Artemis, once loved the handsome giant Orion, who shared her enthusiasm for hunting. But when he was unfaithful to her, she killed him and placed him in the sky as the constellation Orion. In another myth, her slaying of Orion was accidental. She was tricked into it by her brother Apollo, who was jealous of her affection for Orion and wanted to be rid of him.

From these stories you can see that when a god or goddess fell in love, the object of his or her affection had little choice in the matter and might be punished for not returning the immortal's affection. Perhaps the Greek storytellers wanted their listeners to realize that sexual love or infatuation is a wayward emotion, hard to control and unpredictable.

✏️ A CHANCE TO REVIEW

- You have now completed twelve of the lessons in this mythology unit. Today's worksheet is a practice test to see how much you recall from the stories you have read. Again, you are asked to match the name with the appropriate description.

NAME	DESCRIPTION
1. **Pandora's box**	_____ Her gift of prophecy did her little good.
2. **Cassandra**	_____ Like Athena, he was much admired by the Greeks.
3. **Apollo**	_____ This was the dwelling place of the gods.
4. **Ares**	_____ In the creation myth, the principle of order; later, the god of love.
5. **Poseidon**	_____ The Greeks disliked this god.
6. **Orpheus**	_____ Sometimes he is called Earthshaker; his symbols are the trident and dolphin.
7. **Daedalus**	_____ He was the god of wine and intoxication.
8. **Mount Etna**	_____ He stole fire for mankind.
9. **Mount Olympus**	_____ It contained all the woes of the world.
10. **Prometheus**	_____ Hephaestus had his forge here.
11. **Aphrodite**	_____ He was the bravest of the Greek warriors, but he had a vulnerable spot.
12. **Achilles**	_____ She married Hephaestus.
13. **Dionysus**	_____ His music charmed even Hades.
14. **Athena**	_____ He used an ingenious method to escape from a prison.
15. **Cronus**	_____ He stole Persephone from her mother.
16. **Eros**	_____ He made the first woman.
17. **Hades**	_____ Sometimes he is called Cloud Gatherer; he carries thunderbolts.
18. **Hephaestus**	_____ It was like this in the beginning.
19. **Zeus**	_____ She was the goddess of wisdom and a friend of Odysseus.
20. **Chaos**	_____ He is often called Father Time.

Each answer is worth five points. Are you pleased with your score?

PART I WHEN GODS WALKED THE EARTH   LESSON 14

About 800 B.C., the Greek poet Homer wrote two famous epic poems. One, *The Iliad*, was the story of the great war between the Greeks and the Trojans. The other, *The Odyssey*, was the story of one Greek warrior, Odysseus, and his long period of wandering after the Trojan War. These two poems are considered the oldest written literature in the Western world, but we know that a long tradition of oral poetry and storytelling preceded them.

Homer retells some of the myths in his two poems; but *The Iliad* and *The Odyssey* also give us a great deal more information about how the Greeks lived and thought. The reader soon recognizes that the people imagined the gods might be walking among them at any time. Knowing that the gods often assumed human disguises, the Greeks treated all strangers kindly and generously.

For example, a stranger who came to a house was fed and given a chance to bathe before anyone inquired as to his name or business. Upon leaving, the guest was given a "stranger's gift" as a memento of the visit. For the Greeks, hospitality was an art as well as a religious duty.

But, as you have already observed from the myths, the Greeks had their share of human failings. They gradually became lax in their observance of the rules of hospitality. Even worse, they began to neglect to make sacrifices to the gods. At this point, Zeus decided to teach them a lesson. He sent a nine-day deluge to destroy these godless people who had ceased to be reverent.

Only one aged couple survived this terrible flood. They were Deucalion (son of Prometheus) and his wife Pyrrha (daughter of Epimetheus and Pandora). Accounts vary as to why these two were saved. One story is that when Zeus was wandering the earth in disguise, Deucalion and Pyrrha were the only people to show him hospitality. Another myth says that Prometheus warned his son about the impending disaster. Deucalion

then built a great floating chest or ark and stowed enough food in it so that he and Pyrrha could survive until the waters receded.

When the waters did recede, Deucalion and Pyrrha found themselves alone and lonely. Zeus then spoke to Deucalion through an oracle, telling him to cast behind him the bones of his mother. The two old people, puzzled at first, eventually interpreted the advice. The oracle's words referred to Mother Earth, whose bones were the rocks. These they cast over their shoulders. Each one that Pyrrha threw became a woman and each one that Deucalion threw became a man. Thus, in a sense, Deucalion and Pyrrha became the parents of a new race of people, reverent and god-fearing like themselves.

In this story, you've met Zeus in a new guise—as a stern and just father, laying down rules for his people's behavior, punishing those who disobey, and rewarding those who are obedient.

Athena, too, was actively involved with the lives of mortals. In *The Odyssey*, she fights side by side with the hero, Odysseus. She takes a personal interest in Odysseus's son, Telemachus, urging him to action, sometimes by scolding and sometimes by building his confidence. She comforts Odysseus's wife, Penelope. In short, she is a friend and ally to Odysseus and his family.

Zeus and Athena were not the only gods who walked the earth. Demeter also wandered from land to land after she lost Persephone. Dionysus and his followers were believed to inhabit the woodlands, as was Pan, god of the fields and forests. In fact, the Greeks believed spirits existed everywhere—lesser gods than the great Olympians, but immortals all the same. Beautiful, immortal maidens called nymphs lived in mossy glens and flowering fields; and others called naiads lived in sparkling streams. In other words, the gods were part of the natural world.

✎ SOME PARALLELS AND POSERS

1. You have already been asked about Pandora's counterpart in Christian belief. She was Eve, of course. Can you see how Pyrrha might also be seen as Eve's counterpart? Explain.

   _____

   _____

   _____

2. If you look for parallels, you must see that the Deucalion-Pyrrha story also has one in Christian belief. What is it?

   _____

   _____

   _____

3. Long, long ago, a flood actually occurred in the Tigris-Euphrates Valley, a region that is now part of Turkey and Iraq. The Deucalion-Pyrrha myth might have had its origin in that event. You probably remember from Lesson 1 the reasons myths were created. What might be two reasons for this particular myth?

   _____

   _____

   _____

4. Have you ever heard or read anything that might indicate that some people still see natural disasters as a punishment for people's wickedness? Give details.

   _____

   _____

   _____

5. A few years ago, the Mexican government decided to move the centuries-old statue of Tlaloc, the Aztec rain god, from the village where it stood to Mexico City's Museum of Anthropology. At the time the transfer took place, Mexico City had been experiencing a lengthy drought, but the statue's arrival at the museum was marked by three days of torrential rain! Imagine that you are one of the villagers (incidentally, they protested the removal of the statue). How would you account for the sudden rainy spell?

   _____

   _____

   _____

PART I

MYTHS AND MORALS

LESSON 15

In completing the worksheet for Lesson 14, you probably noted that the story of Deucalion and Pyrrha can be classified as a "scientific" myth. That is, it explains an actual phenomenon, a terrible flood. But the story is also a myth with a moral. It shows that evildoers are punished and god-fearing people are rewarded.

Now, see if you can discover a moral in each of the following myths.

In Greek mythology, a god never broke a promise, once given, even while knowing disaster might follow. Such was the case with Helios, the sun god, and his young son Phaeton (sometimes said to be the son of Apollo). Without considering the consequences, Helios once told Phaeton that he would grant any request the boy made. Rashly, Phaeton asked to drive the sun god's chariot across the heavens. In vain, Helios tried to dissuade him. Phaeton insisted.

Of course, the boy soon lost control of the spirited horses, and the chariot plunged wildly, first toward heaven, then toward earth. There, the sun's heat dried up the rivers and scorched the earth, creating deserts. To stop this terrible destruction, Zeus sent a thunderbolt which struck poor Phaeton and sent him to his death.

Unlike the inexperienced youth Phaeton, Bellerophon was a hero who accomplished many difficult tasks with the aid of the remarkable flying horse Pegasus, whom Athena had sent to help him. But Bellerophon literally tried to fly too high when he asked Pegasus to carry him to the heavens. Pegasus was stung by a gadfly, threw his rider to his death, and flew up to heaven alone.

Echo was a beautiful mountain nymph whose only fault was a tendency to talk too much. Jealous Hera suspected that the nymph's incessant chatter was a deliberate attempt to distract her so that Zeus would be free to give his attention to other females. To punish Echo, Hera decreed that she could never again speak until spoken to and then could simply echo what she had heard.

But poor Echo's troubles were only beginning. She fell in love with a handsome youth, Narcissus, who scorned her. Brokenhearted, Echo hid away in the mountains. Now, only her voice remains. But Narcissus was punished for his coldness and indifference. Aphrodite made him fall in love with his own image, which he found reflected in a pool. He continued to stare at it until, consumed by self-love, he fell into the pool and was drowned.

✎ YOU HAVE THE LAST WORD

• Supply the appropriate word or words to complete the following statements.

1. Phaeton's fault was _____ .

2. In the myths, another boy who got into trouble because he wouldn't take his father's

   advice was _____ .

3. The Helios-Phaeton myth explains why the deserts have no _____ .

4. Bellerophon's fault was _____ .

5. Bellerophon had something in common with Phaeton because each wanted to

   _____ .

6. Echo's only fault was her _____ .

7. Echo hid away because she was _____ .

8. Narcissus came to a bad end because he was too much _____ .

9. Briefly state what the following expression means and relate it to one of the myths
   you know.

   He's trying to fly too high.

   _____

   _____

   _____

   _____

   _____

   _____

10. Use the dictionary to find the meaning of the word hubris. Be ready to tell the class how it
    applies to Phaeton, Bellerophon, and Narcissus.

PART I **HADES'S KINGDOM, THE UNDERWORLD** LESSON 16

You may remember from Lesson 9, which introduced you to Zeus and his brothers, that the Greeks were reluctant to mention Hades's name because they thought with dread of their final descent into his kingdom.

The myths tell us what they imagined the Underworld was like. Generally, it was a gloomy place where the sun never shone. People who had been neither very good nor very bad on earth became shadows or shades who wandered about aimlessly. They could feel emotion and could speak, but their bodies had no substance.

Not all of Hades's realm was quite so grim. The heroes and others whose goodness had distinguished them on earth were sent to the Elysian Fields, a place of sunlight and flowers. But for the Greeks, even the Elysian Fields were a disappointment compared with life on earth. In *The Odyssey*, the spirit of the great warrior Achilles talks with Odysseus, who has ventured into the Underworld, and tells him that he'd rather be the humblest man alive than be a hero and dwell in Hades's kingdom.

The third section of the Underworld was Tartarus, a sunless hole where those whose life on earth had been wicked endured eternal punishments. It was here that Tantalus reached forever toward the food and drink that always remained just beyond his grasp. Here too, Sisyphus struggled constantly to push a huge boulder to the top of a hill, only to see it roll back to the bottom

once more. And here Ixion was bound forever to a constantly revolving wheel.

The Underworld was a place of mountains and valleys, just like earth itself, but it had several remarkable rivers. The first of these, the Styx, was the boundary between the world of the living and the world of the dead. Charon, the boatman, ferried the souls across this river to Hades, if they had proper funeral rites and had the fare. Otherwise, they were doomed to wander on the far shore for one hundred years.

Acheron, the river of woe, was another of the rivers surrounding Hades. The souls of the dead had to be ferried across it also or struggle through it themselves. Into the Acheron flowed the Cocytus, the river of wailing, and the Phlegethon, the river of fire. This last river actually surrounded Tartarus. Finally, there was Lethe, the river of forgetfulness. Those passing into the Elysian Fields drank its water to help them cast off earthly sorrows.

The actual entrance to Hades was guarded by Cerberus, the three-headed dog, who was constantly watchful; even if two of his three heads were sleeping, the third was always awake.

Details of the geography of Hades evolved, as the myths evolved through the centuries. But on one point, all stories seemed to agree—even at its best in the Elysian Fields, existence in Hades did not compare favorably with life on earth.

© 1984, 1997 J. Weston Walch, Publisher   *Mythology: A Teaching Unit*

✎ THINKING IT OVER

1. How do the Christian concepts of heaven and hell differ from the Greeks' idea of Hades?

   _____

   _____

   _____

2. What seemed to be the best way for a Greek to make certain to be assigned to the Elysian Fields?

   _____

   _____

   _____

3. Tartarus seems to resemble our idea of hell. Does Hades in any way resemble Satan? Explain.

   _____

   _____

   _____

4. **Vocabulary**

• All of the following words are derived from words in today's lesson. (One of the words you have already met in an earlier lesson.) Write a definition beside each word you know. Then use the dictionary to check your definitions and complete the exercise.

   WORD   DEFINITION

   A. **lethargic**   _____

   B. **lethal**   _____

   C. **tantalize**   _____

   D. **Elysian**   _____

   E. **shade**   _____

PART I   **DEATH AND IMMORTALITY**   LESSON 17

You know now that the Greeks believed the souls of those who had died all descended to Hades. There, three judges, Aeacus, Minos, and Rhadamanthus, decided to what section each would be assigned, taking into consideration the person's behavior on earth.

Apparently, the souls could still eat and drink, speak, and feel emotion or pain. In Elysium (another name for the Elysian Fields) they could live almost as they had on earth, yet be free of all earthly worries. Still, they apparently found their unearthly existence dull.

How did the Greeks know all this? Because some of the heroes of the myths descended into Hades and then managed to return to the land of the living. One of these was Orpheus, whom you have already met. His love for his bride, Eurydice, was so strong that he went down to the Underworld to rescue her. Symbolically, then, love seemed to be conquering death—at least until Orpheus looked backward and, through that small act of disobedience, lost Eurydice forever.

Odysseus also visited the Underworld. His objective was to seek the advice of the blind prophet Tiresias and find out how, having once offended Poseidon, he could still make his way by ship back to his home in Ithaca.

In the Underworld, Odysseus talked to his own mother, Anticleia, who had died during his long absence. But when he tried to embrace her, he realized that she was only a shadow. He also saw the other heroes of the Trojan War and talked to them. Agamemnon told him how his wife had betrayed him. Achilles asked about his son, Neoptolemus; Odysseus told him that the boy fought bravely.

Odysseus gained knowledge from each shade he talked to, and he left the Underworld determined to follow Tiresias's advice and to avoid all pitfalls on his journey home. If his men had not disobeyed him and eaten the sacred cattle of Helios, he could have brought them safely home, too. Symbolically, then, Odysseus's journey to Hades's kingdom was to gain understanding so that he could help his crew (his people) who were dependent on him.

In earlier lessons, you read that both Apollo and Dionysus also went down into darkness (death, the Underworld) and rose again. Dionysus actually succeeded in releasing his mother, Semele, from Hades's kingdom. Thus, since Semele represented all green, growing things, life triumphed over death.

There was another part of the Greek belief Just as Semele escaped from Hades, a chosen few might eventually leave the Elysian Fields, assume their human forms again, and return to life on earth.

PART I   WORSHEET 17

 A SECRET MESSAGE FROM THE UNDERWORLD

- Fill in each blank with the name that fits the description. Then write the first letter of each name in the corresponding numbered space to find the secret message. Blank spaces indicate separations between words.

SECRET MESSAGE

$\overline{}\,\overline{}\,\overline{}\,\overline{}\,\overline{}\quad\overline{}\,\overline{}\,\overline{}\quad\overline{}\,\overline{}\,\overline{}\,\overline{}\,\overline{}\,\overline{}\quad\overline{}\,\overline{}\quad\overline{}\,\overline{}\,\overline{}\,\overline{}\,\overline{}\quad\overline{}\,\overline{}\,\overline{}\,\overline{}\,\overline{}$
1 2 3 4 5   6 7 8   9 10 11 12 13 14   15 16   17 18 19 20 21   22 23 24 25 26

1. _____   Cerberus, who had three heads, naturally had three _____ .

2. _A_____   He was one of the judges in Hades.

3. _____   He was the boatman on the Styx.

4. _____   Her husband almost brought her back to life.

5. _____   He constantly pushed a boulder up a hill.

6. _____   She was the mother of Odysseus.

7. _____   He was the son of Achilles.

8. _Dis_____   In some mythologies, this was the name of the Underworld or its god (name supplied, not in your lesson).

9. _____   The river of fire in Hades, it flowed into the river of woe.

10. _____   This was the river of forgetfulness.

11. _____   Odysseus learned that this hero's wife had deceived him.

12. _____   He was the three-headed dog that guarded the gates of Hades.

13. _Elpenor_   A member of Odysseus's crew, he begs Odysseus in Hades to give him proper funeral rites (name supplied, not in your lesson).

14. _____   This was the river of darkness where Charon was boatman.

15. _____   He was bound to a revolving wheel.

16. _____   That son of Achilles, from 7.

17. _____   He was god of the Underworld.

18. _____   Another of the rivers of Hades, this was the river of woe.

19. _____   He rescued his mother from the Underworld.

20. _____   This was the most desirable part of the Underworld.

21. _____   She represented verdure, everything that was green and growing.

22. _R_____   He was one of the judges of Hades.

23. _____   Same as 4, the wife of Orpheus.

24. _____   He asked Odysseus for news of his son.

25. _____   Same as 10.

26. _____   He was the third Underworld judge.

THE HERO, A REPRESENTATION OF ALL VIRTUES

By now, you must be aware that the Greeks gave their mythical heroes almost the same reverence that they gave their gods. What's more, they believed that even after death, heroes should and did enjoy special privileges.

Certain qualities set the hero apart from ordinary men: He was strong, brave, clever, and determined; he was an effective leader, concerned for his followers' welfare, merciful to them, but merciless to his enemies. Every hero possessed all of these traits to a degree, but each hero was distinguished by one special quality.

The perfect example of the strong man was Hercules (Greek name: Heracles—best known by his Roman name, Hercules). The tales of his remarkable, superhuman feats are among the most fascinating myths.

Since Hercules was the son of Zeus and Alcmene, it was inevitable that Hera, Zeus's jealous wife, would be his enemy. She started her harassment early by sending two snakes to destroy Hercules when he was an infant. But when his mother and his foster father heard a commotion in the room where Hercules and his half brother were sleeping, they rushed in to find the young hero strangling the snakes with his bare hands.

As a young man, Hercules showed his great bravery when he strangled a fierce lion that had been attacking his foster father's sheep. The animal's hide became an ancient Greek version of the bulletproof vest. Hercules wore it as a tunic which no weapon could pierce.

Hercules's life was made miserable by another of Hera's cruelties. In a fit of insanity which she brought upon him, he killed his own children. In atonement for that terrible deed, he performed the famous Twelve Labors of Hercules, a series of seemingly superhuman tasks.

In the Sixth Labor, cleaning the stables of King Augeas, Hercules showed his ingenuity. He was assigned to finish the job in one day. On the surface that might not seem too difficult, but no one had cleaned those stables in thirty years! Hercules solved his problem and met his deadline by diverting a river through the stables.

Hercules's persistence, or determination, is best shown by the Fourth Labor, the capture of the Cerynean Stag, a deer with golden horns who could run continuously and never tire. That labor took Hercules a year to complete, but he succeeded.

You will remember that it was Hercules who mercifully released Prometheus from his bondage. But Hercules could be merciless to his enemies; it was an act of anger against an enemy that eventually caused his own death.

When the centaur Nessus made advances to Hercules's wife, Deianira, Hercules killed him. Before he died, the centaur gave Deianira a few drops of his blood, claiming it would keep Hercules ever faithful to her. Suspecting that her husband was interested in another princess, Deianira dipped his robe in the centaur's blood and sent it to him. Its poisons seared Hercules's body so badly that he begged to be placed on a funeral pyre and welcomed death.

But Hercules's life did not end there. His body was borne to Olympus, where he could be eternally with the gods. Thus, the hero's last great feat was cheating death.

✎ THINKING IT OVER

1. What did each of the following figures from American history or myth have in common with the ancient Greek hero Hercules? *Clue:* Review the qualities of an ancient hero mentioned in this lesson. You may need to do some library research on the two frontiersman and the lumberjack.

   A. Frontiersman Daniel Boone

   _____

   _____

   B. Frontiersman Davy Crockett

   _____

   _____

   C. The mythical lumberjack Paul Bunyan

   _____

   _____

2. How did each of the two heroes, Hercules and Achilles, become almost invincible?

   _____

   _____

   _____

3. What characters in comic books, cartoons, or advertising do you think might be based on Hercules?

   _____

   _____

   _____

4. Consider the following events in Hercules's life.

   A. Zeus, the supreme god, was his father.
   B. Hera sent snakes to destroy him when he was an infant, and he had to struggle with them. Actually, wasn't he being punished for the deeds of others?
   C. While completing one of the Twelve Labors, he relieved Atlas and carried the weight of the world on his shoulders. Symbolically, he carried all its troubles on his shoulders.
   D. He died, was reborn, and went up to Olympus.

• Can you see similarities between the life of this hero from ancient Greece and the life of Christ in the Christian tradition? Explain.

   _____

   _____

PART I   LESSON 19

THE HEROES PERSEUS AND THESEUS

When an oracle told King Acrisius that he would have no son and that his grandson would kill him, Acrisius locked up his only daughter, Danaë, figuring that if she had no suitors, he would have no grandson. But locked doors could not keep out Zeus. He appeared to lovely Danaë as a shower of gold, and she bore him a son, Perseus.

After the king discovered what had happened, he set his daughter and her baby adrift on the sea. The two were rescued, however, and taken to King Polydectes, in whose kingdom Perseus grew up. By then, Polydectes had decided he wanted Danaë for his wife, so he decided to get rid of Perseus by sending him on a seemingly impossible quest. He sent Perseus to bring back the head of Medusa, one of three horrible sisters called Gorgons. Medusa had snakes for hair, and her glance was so terrible that anyone who looked directly at her was instantly turned to stone.

The gods helped Perseus by sending him first to the Graiai, or Gray-Eyed Ones, three strange sisters who shared one eye and one tooth among them. By stealing their eye and tooth, Perseus forced them to tell him the whereabouts of the magic helmet, sandals, and pouch he needed for his quest.

Another god-provided prop, a magic mirror, made it possible for him to cut off Medusa's head without looking directly at her. Stowing the head in the magic pouch, he began his return journey. On his way home, he rescued a beautiful princess, Andromeda, whose father was offering her to a sea monster that had been threatening the kingdom. Making use of the winged sandals, Perseus attacked the monster from above, killed it, and carried away Andromeda as his bride.

Home at last, the hero used Medusa's head to turn Polydectes and his court to stone, and then he rescued his mother. Eventually, he did kill his grandfather by accident, proving that the fate foretold by the oracle could not be avoided.

The hero Theseus showed his great strength early. Before leaving home, Theseus's father had hidden a sword and sandals under a huge boulder, telling his wife to let their son remove them when he was able. After young Theseus had accomplished that feat, he went on to Athens and performed other deeds of strength and courage, thus becoming a special hero to the Athenians.

At that time, the Athenians were forced to pay a yearly tribute of seven young men and seven young women to Minos, King of Crete. Minos would imprison them in the labyrinth that Daedalus had built for him. But imprisonment was not all that these poor Athenians suffered. In the maze, Minos kept a strange and fearsome animal, half man and half bull, called the Minotaur. Eventually, it ate anyone imprisoned there.

In selfless fashion, Theseus decided to halt this horrible slaughter of the innocents. He went to Crete, entered the labyrinth, and slew the monster. But he might have remained Minos's prisoner if the king's daughter, Ariadne, had not given him a ball of twine. Theseus unraveled the twine as he walked through the labyrinth and then used it to retrace his steps. When Theseus left Crete, he took Ariadne with him; but unfortunately he later abandoned her.

Name _____ Date _____

 # ANALYZING THE HEROES' ACTIONS

- In an earlier lesson, you read that all the heroes possessed certain characteristics in common—in a sense, they were all poured from the same mold. These characteristics are listed in Column A. Column B contains brief descriptions of certain acts of either Perseus or Theseus. You are asked to decide which characteristic is best revealed by each act. Then place the letter corresponding to it in the space provided beside each act.

COLUMN A	COLUMN B
CHARACTERISTICS	ACTIONS
B. **bravery**	1. _____ Perseus's stealing the Graiai's eye and tooth
A. **strength**	2. _____ Theseus's moving the boulder to get the sword and sandals
C. **cleverness**	3. _____ Theseus's decision to go to Crete to kill the Minotaur
D. **persistence or determination**	4. _____ Perseus's willingness to go on the quest to get the Gorgon's head
E. **mercy to the weak**	5. _____ Perseus's using the magic mirror to avoid looking at Medusa
F. **mercilessness to enemies**	6. _____ Perseus's rescue of Andromeda
	7. _____ Perseus's use of the Gorgon's head to turn Polydectes and his court to stone
G. **selflessness**	8. _____ Ariadne's showing Theseus a way to get out of the maze

9. Hercules's outstanding trait was his great strength. What do you think was the outstanding trait of Perseus? of Theseus? Explain your choices.

   _____

   _____

10. In the accounts of Perseus and Theseus, what do you think the fate of Ariadne, Danaë, and Andromeda indicates about the status of women in ancient Greece?

   _____

   _____

PART I

LESSON 20

ACHILLES AND ODYSSEUS, HOMER'S WARRIOR-HEROES

In the long poems *The Iliad* and *The Odyssey*, the ancient Greek poet Homer makes the heroes Achilles and Odysseus so believable that readers are inclined to judge their actions just as they might judge people they know. A few incidents from their stories follow. After you have read them, you may decide that you like one hero better than the other.

◆ ◆ ◆

In the 24 books (chapters) of *The Iliad*, which is the story of the Trojan War, Achilles inspires his comrades with his bravery. Unfortunately, he quarrels with the commanding general, Agamemnon, who has taken a fancy to Achilles's slave girl and wants her for himself. Sulkily, Achilles withdraws from battle and remains in his tent. Without him, the Greeks' morale is so low that the tide of battle turns in the Trojans' favor.

Achilles's best friend then borrows his armor and goes onto the battlefield, hoping the Trojans will mistake him for Achilles and lose courage. The trick works, but Achilles' friend is killed by the Trojan prince Hector. Wild with grief, Achilles vows revenge; but he must have armor before he can go onto the battlefield.

At this point, Achilles's mother, Thetis, intervenes. You may recall that when he was an infant, she had dipped him in the River Styx, hoping to make him invulnerable. Ever protective, she had tried to prevent him from entering the Trojan War because it had been prophesied that he would die on the battlefield. Now, she persuades Hephaestus to make new armor for him. Wearing it, Achilles charges onto the battlefield, driving the Trojans before him.

Only Hector refuses to retreat behind the city walls. Achilles now takes his revenge. Three times he chases Hector around the walls of Troy, at last killing him with a spear. Fierce in his anger and grief, he then drags Hector's body three times more around those walls for all the Trojans to see. But, in a more merciful mood, he later releases

the body to Hector's father, King Priam, and declares a temporary truce for the funeral rites.

◆ ◆ ◆

Odysseus, the hero of *The Odyssey*, is very different from Achilles. He is less emotional, less impetuous, more clever and crafty, less merciful, and more foolhardy.

Because he offends the gods in two ways, by stealing the statue of Athena from Troy and by blinding Poseidon's one-eyed son, the Cyclops Polyphemos, he is doomed to trials and tribulations on his long journey home from the Trojan War.

In the Cyclops incident, Odysseus lingers at Polyphemos's cave to get his "stranger's gift," even though his men beg him to leave. This costs him several followers, whom the Cyclops eats. But through Odysseus's cleverness, the remaining men escape from the cave where Polyphemos has held them prisoner. As they sail away, however, Odysseus taunts the now-blind giant. Polyphemos retaliates by throwing rocks at the ship, almost causing disaster for Odysseus and his crew.

Unlike Agamemnon and Achilles, who argued over the slave girl, Odysseus seems relatively indifferent to the women he meets and determined to return to his wife, Penelope. He eventually leaves the beautiful witches Circe and Calypso and declines to marry the lovely princess Nausicaa.

When he finally arrives home, he finds Penelope still faithful to him, kills all the false suitors who have been trying to marry her, and murders all the female servants who have not been loyal to him and their mistress.

During his journey, Odysseus goes down into the Underworld and returns, determined to appease Poseidon. In fact, throughout his travels he remains obedient to the gods. Homer has made him the most complex and human of heroes. Odysseus called himself "Noman." He is every man.

✎ IF THE ANCIENTS ADVERTISED

- Imagine there was a mythological newspaper, The Olympian Gazette. Who might have placed each of the following ads? Fill in the space beside the ad with the appropriate name from the list below.

POSSIBLE ADVERTISERS

Augeas	**Perseus**	**Tiresias**	**Thetis**
Andromeda	**Minos**	**Graiai**	**Ariadne**
Danaë	**Odysseus**	**Sirens**	**Theseus**
Penelope	**Polyphemos**		

ADVERTISEMENT—HELP WANTED

1. _____ Needed at once, sea-monster exterminator.

2. _____ Master carpenter and designer, labyrinth experience a must.

3. _____ General handyman, strong and willing to clean stables, handle other odd jobs.

4. _____ Highly skilled metalworker, armor experience. Highest rate for quick work.

5. _____ Desperately needed, locksmith, to free princess from tower.

SITUATIONS WANTED

6. _____ Attractive young woman, currently unemployed, seeks position as Girl Friday. Good at puzzle solving, knows a few rope and string tricks.

7. _____ Storyteller available for parties, etc. Widely traveled, has personal knowledge of witches, monsters, sirens.

8. _____ Handicapped person, best of recommendations, offers advice to travelers, provided you can come to me.

9. _____ Bullfighter, experienced, no maze too difficult for me to escape.

10. _____ Talented group of female singers seeking employment. Give us an audition. You may find us irresistible.

MISSING PRESONS

11. _____ Loving husband, now absent nearly twenty years. Would be grateful for any information as to his whereabouts.

12. _____ Need information about three women, sometimes known as "The Gray Ones." Important business proposition involved.

LOST AND FOUND

13. _____ Lost, one eye and one tooth, under peculiar circumstances. Generous reward offered.

WANTED TO BUY OR RENT

14. _____ Glass eye. Cannot pay cash, but willing to give equal value in sheep and cheese.

15. _____ Winged sandals and specially constructed helmet. Needed for one job only. Guarantee to return in good condition.

PART I   LESSON 21

THE GODS OF GREECE MEET THE GODS OF ROME

When Rome gained the supremacy of the ancient world, the old Greek gods survived, but the Romans renamed them and changed their characters somewhat. Whereas the Greek divinities had both good and bad qualities, the Romans tended to see each of their gods as representative of a particular virtue. Thus, the gods became more remote from the people as they became examples of unattainable perfection.

Zeus, now renamed Jupiter, was still the supreme deity—the protector of the state, guardian of law, and defender of truth and virtue. He controlled the lives of human beings, but he never came down to earth to mingle with the people. His wife, Juno (Hera), was a protectress of women in general and especially of women during childbirth.

Athena's Roman name was Minerva. She was still a warrior-goddess, a goddess of wisdom, and a patroness of handcrafts. Along with Jupiter and Juno, she was worshiped in a temple on the Capitoline Hill in Rome.

Mars (Ares) was held in higher esteem by the Romans, a warlike people, than he had been by the Greeks. He was honored through festivals and sacrifices; the month of March was named for him; he was reputed to be the father of Romulus and Remus, the mythical founders of Rome; and he was second in importance only to Jupiter.

Venus's role in Roman mythology was almost identical with Aphrodite's in the Greek myths. She was the goddess of love and beauty; Mars was her lover. But she was also a nature goddess who caused the flowers to bloom in the spring. In addition, she was a protectress of Rome.

Pluto (Hades) was to the Romans the ruler of the dead and a giver of wealth—remember that Hades was guardian of all the treasures (minerals) under the earth. Pluto's wife, Proserpina, was the equivalent of the Greek Persephone.

Neptune was originally the god of moisture who filled the springs and streams. In later myths, like the Greek Poseidon, he was god of the sea.

Diana, like Artemis, was the moon goddess and the goddess of forests and hunting. Like Juno, she was a protectress of women in childbirth.

Apollo, the sun god, was worshiped by the Romans as he had been by the Greeks. You will remember that Apollo had the sun's power to heal. When, in the fifth century B.C., Rome was threatened by a plague, the people adopted Apollo as their own, hoping to receive his healing powers.

But the Romans also had an ancient sun deity of their own; he was Janus, the god with two faces—one looking backward, the other forward. Appropriately, Janus's name was given to the first month of the year. A temple and archway were dedicated to him. Roman soldiers marching off to war went through the arch to gain his special protection. His temple gates remained always open in wartime and closed in peacetime. Only three closings occurred in seven hundred years!

Ceres, goddess of the harvest, was the Roman counterpart of Demeter. Vesta, goddess of the hearth and protectress of the sacred altar fire, was like the Greek Hestia. In Vesta's temple, six virgins from noble Roman families guarded the sacred fire at all times.

Mercury was the Roman Hermes, god of commerce. On May 15, his festival day, merchandise was sprinkled with sacred water to guarantee high profits.

Vulcan, god of fire and of volcanoes (think of where Hephaestus's forge was located), was just like Hephaestus.

Bacchus, like Dionysus, was a god of fertility and wine. His sacred rituals were called Bacchanalia; gradually, they changed into orgies, causing his name to be associated with drunkenness. Of the Roman gods, Bacchus unfortunately became the most human.

✎ THE MATCH GAME

- From your study of this lesson, supply the Roman name of the god or goddess who fits each of the following descriptions. Use your memory, and do not look back at the lesson until you have filled in as many blanks as possible.

1. _____ He was a two-faced sun god.
2. _____ To tend her sacred fire was a great honor.
3. _____ Pluto carried her daughter down into his kingdom.
4. _____ He was the remote and majestic source of law and order.
5. _____ Roman matrons looked up to her as an example of womanhood and as their protectress.
6. _____ Sacred rituals in his honor became too frenzied.
7. _____ He helped people to "turn a profit."
8. _____ His power as a healer made him a universal god.
9. _____ His temple gates were seldom closed.
10. _____ She ruled the night sky, as her brother Apollo ruled the day sky.
11. _____ She was Jupiter's wise warrior daughter.
12. _____ The Romans gave him honors he never earned from the Greeks.
13. _____ He made the sparks fly.
14. _____ He was the god of wealth, but he was also a kidnapper.
15. _____ He was lord of the sea.

- Now for some easy vocabulary sleuthing. From whose name was each of the following words derived?

16. _____ merchandise
17. _____ merchant
18. _____ merciful
19. _____ March
20. _____ January
21. _____ Jovian
22. _____ mercurial
23. _____ martial
24. _____ Junoesque

- Now use the dictionary to find the meaning of any of the above words in numbers 16 through 24 that are not familiar to you.

PART I **THE ZODIAC, THE CIRCLE OF LIFE** LESSON 22

Do you check your horoscope each day in the newspaper? Do you believe what you read there? If you are not sure, you share your doubts with many people over many centuries. Yet interest in astrology remains strong.

The word *horoscope* comes from the Greek words *hora* for "hour" and *skopas* meaning "watcher" or "observer." Thus, your horoscope is based on observation of the position of the planets and stars in relation to one another at the hour of your birth. Obviously, the daily newspaper predictions are general, for anyone born under a particular sign of the zodiac. But by the law of averages, sometimes a horoscope will have a message or advice that seems to be meant only for you.

The zodiac, or circle of life (actually, in Greek, circle of animals) is the basis for the horoscope. Divided into twelve parts to correspond to the twelve cycles the moon makes around the earth annually, each part of the zodiac is named for a constellation.

How did the zodiac come to exist? Astrology, the interest in and observation of heavenly bodies, is very ancient. The Babylonians observed that in addition to the fixed stars in the heavens there were certain other stars that moved. They had their own names for these wanderers, but the Greeks later called them planets. They consisted of the sun and moon, plus Jupiter, Mars, Mercury, Saturn, and Venus. You will notice that the last five are names of Roman gods; it was once thought that the planets were gods.

The early astrologers observed that the planets moved only through a narrow band of the sky, marked by twelve constellations. These constellations, which became the signs of the zodiac, were believed to be the houses of the planet gods.

Those ancient scientists discovered that the planets moved according to a predictable pattern. Thus, they reasoned, if the events in the heavens followed a pattern, that pattern would be reflected in events on the earth. For the individual, the position of the planets at the time of birth would determine what the future would hold. Each person's destiny was in the hands of the gods (the planets). In this way, the use of astrology to predict the future began.

However, the zodiacal sign not only determined a person's future, but also was a clue to character—or so the ancients believed.

Aries, the ram, was the first sign of the zodiac, since the sun's entrance into the house of Aries corresponded to the spring equinox, approximately March 22. It was believed that people born under this sign would be courageous, energetic, and impetuous.

Leo, the lion, was thought to confer dignity and power on those born under his sign. The sun entered the house of Leo in midsummer when its rays ' were most powerful. Each of the other constellations was responsible for certain human characteristics, at least in astrological lore.

The planets, too, had an influence on human behavior. Such words as moonstruck, saturnine, and mercurial all had their origin in this belief. Thus a moonstruck person is deranged because of the influence of the moon, a saturnine disposition is basically grave and gloomy, and a mecurial one is changeable.

In Shakespeare's *Julius Caesar*, Cassius tells Brutus, "The fault, dear Brutus, is not in our stars, but in ourselves that we are underlings." In *Romeo and Juliet*, the two young people are "star-cross'd lovers," indicating that perhaps their astrological signs were not compatible.

Have you ever called a teacher crabby? That adjective comes from Cancer the crab, another sign of the zodiac. Does anyone you know own a Ford Taurus, named for yet another sign? And are you still planning to check your horoscope tomorrow? If you do, remember that you are following an ancient tradition.

PART I   WORKSHEET 22

✎ A CLOSE LOOK AT WORDS

- Let's see how well you understood the three planet-related words you learned in today's lesson. Write a sentence for each of the following words. Try not to use forms of the verb to be (is, am, are, etc.)

    1. **mecurial** (adjective) _____

    _____

    2. **moonstruck** (adjective) _____

    _____

    3. **saturnine** (adjective) _____

    _____

    4. List two words besides *horoscope* that have *scope* for a suffix. Example: *telescope. Clue:* Try the medical field.

    5. In the quotation from *Julius Caesar,* "The fault, dear Brutus, is not in our stars, but in ourselves that we are underlings," does Cassius seem to be accepting the theory that the planets and stars control our destiny? Explain.

    _____

    6. The Greek word that is anglicized as *planet* actually meant *wanderer.* Why did they choose that word to describe those seven particular stars?

    _____

PART I   **THE PRINCIPAL NORSE GODS** LESSON 23

Think about Monday morning. If you wake up to brilliant sunshine, the world seems a very happy place, and the prospect of a week crammed with homework, tests, and practice sessions seems challenging. Change that sunshine to lowering clouds or gray rain, and you crawl out of bed, discouraged before you start. The weather affects our moods, our capacity for work, even our way of looking at the world. Naturally, people living in a northern climate where winter brings long hours of darkness, biting winds, and deep snow would develop a gloomier world view than did the Greeks in their sun-drenched country with its mild climate.

Norse myths, the oral history of the Scandinavian people, are melancholy. The overall mood is of impending doom—no matter how hard people strive in this world, death will bring them ultimate defeat. Not even the gods are exempt from this destruction. The Norse imagined a kind of doomsday, Ragnarok (the Twilight of the Gods), which would be preceded by a breakdown of morality and an increase in lawlessness. Then Ragnarok would signal a battle between the evil Loki, allied with the giants, and the gods. Destruction would be complete: the sun, moon, and stars would disappear; the world would perish in fire.

Truly a gloomy prospect, but there was some hope. Balder, the best-loved god, would then be reincarnated, and two human beings would survive the destruction of Ragnarok. A new race of people would begin, a new sun would give more heat and light, and life on earth would be better than before.

That was the future as the Norse saw it. What of the past? First, they believed in a rather strange universe. At the time of creation, Jutenheim, a region of ice and snow, became the home of the frost giants. Human beings (created from ash and elm trees by the god Odin) lived on earth or Midgard, encircled by the Midgard Serpent, a personification of the ocean. Below earth was Darkalfheim, home of the gnomes. Above earth was Asgard, home of the gods, protected from the giants by a huge wall and connected to earth by the Rainbow Bridge, Bifrost.

Several other regions existed, and connecting all regions was the World Tree, Yggdrasil. It had roots in Jutenheim, Midgard, and Asgard. Symbolically, it was the Tree of Life, but it was not indestructible. The tree required the constant attention of the Norns, three giantesses who lived beneath it, to keep it from decay.

Two other important regions were Hel, the abode of those who had died from sickness or old age, and Valhalla, the abode of the heroes who had died in battle. Their bodies were taken from the battlefield and carried to Valhalla by the Valkyries—beautiful, goldenhaired warrior-maidens.

Odin was the chief Norse god—creator of human beings, ruler of Valhalla, and god of wisdom. Through self-sacrifice (he gave up an eye) he had gained wisdom and thus his power. From his name comes the word Wodensday, or Wednesday. His wife, Frigga, was a kindly goddess, protectress of women in childbirth, patroness of love and marriage, and a fertility goddess to whom childless couples could appeal. From her name or from that of Freya (goddess of love) comes the word Friday.

Thor, the thunder god, was the son of Odin. With his magic belt, hammer, and gloves, he was able to slay monsters and frost giants. You can guess what day of the week took its name from his.

Brave Tyr was the god of battle. He sacrificed a hand in order to chain the wolf Fenrir, who was a threat to the gods.

Loki was the troublemaker among the gods and human beings. His gifts to the first human beings were desires and passions, gifts not guaranteed to produce serenity. He fathered the fierce wolf Fenrir. He was responsible for the death of Balder. He was changeable, a trickster, and a thief.

Loki's opposite was Balder the Good, son of Odin and Frigga. His mother made everything in the world—rocks, plants, and trees—promise not to hurt him, but she forgot to get a promise from the mistletoe, and a mistletoe arrow caused his death. His resurrection, after Ragnarok, would signal the beginning of a Golden Age for the Norse.

© 1984, 1997 J. Weston Walch, Publisher   *Mythology: A Teaching Unit*

✎ SOME SIMILARITIES AND DIFFERENCES

1. To protect her son Balder, Frigga went to great lengths, asking the very stones on the ground to do him no harm. What other mythical mother was equally devoted and vigilant?

   _____

   _____

2. Balder was vulnerable only to the mistletoe dart, and it caused his death. What Greek hero's story does Balder's death bring to your mind?

   _____

   _____

3. The slain Norse heroes went to Valhalla, a place of feasting and freedom from pain. What is the parallel in the Greek myths?

   _____

   _____

4. Why would the frost giants be depicted as so threatening in the Norse myths?

   _____

   _____

5. Why would the Norse hope for a Golden Age to come, when the sun would give more heat and light?

   _____

   _____

6. With the exception of Loki, who has no exact counterpart in the Greek myths, how does each of the following Norse gods described seem different from the corresponding Greek god (in parentheses)? *Clue:* Keep in mind Odin's and Tyr's self-sacrifice, Balder's general goodness, and Frigga's kindly attitude toward human beings.

   Balder (Apollo) _____

   Odin (Zeus) _____

   Frigga (Hera) _____

   Tyr (Ares) _____

7. Does the fact that the very gods and life itself (the Tree of Life) could be destroyed suggest anything to you about the Norse view of the world? Explain.

   _____

   _____

   _____

© 1984, 1997 J. Weston Walch, Publisher   *Mythology: A Teaching Unit*

PART I   LESSON 24

YGGDRASIL, THE NORSE TREE OF LIFE

In the Garden of Eden, the fruit of only one tree, the Tree of Knowledge, was forbidden to Adam and Eve. But the serpent tempted Eve. She and Adam ate the apple and thus lost their innocence. For their disobedience, God banished them forever from the Garden of Eden.

The tree was symbolic, of course, and a symbolic tree is part of many mythologies. For the Celts, it was the sacred oak of the Druids. In the *Odyssey*, it was the tree from which Odysseus carved his marriage bed, the tree that remained firmly rooted in his house. In Christian belief, the Tree of Jesse is actually the family record of Christ. And when we talk of our family tree, we mean our personal tree of life.

No other mythology has a more remarkable tree than the Norse Yggdrasil, a sturdy ash. In Lesson 23, you read a bit about its three roots, the first embedded in Jutenheim, the land of the frost giants; the second, in Midgard, the land of human beings; and the third, in Asgard, home of the Aesir gods including Odin, Thor, Balder, and Loki, among others. In another version, the second root ends in Niflheim, a land of mist and darkness. In that version, it was one of the tree's branches that reached the land of mankind.

More significant than the geography of Yggdrasil are other details that reveal more of the Norse point of view. The first root, which went down to the land of the frost giants, also concealed the spring of Mimir, the god of wisdom. It was to Mimir that Odin gave one of his eyes in return for drinking from the spring and gaining knowledge. Realizing that knowledge

was power, Odin made another self-sacrifice. He used his own spear to hang himself (temporarily, of course) on Yggdrasil, for he wanted to learn the runes, a magic alphabet. He remained impaled for nine days until the runic letters appeared on the leaves of the tree. Thus he acquired the art of writing, since he now had an alphabet, and he acquired some magical powers as well. Since Odin was first among the Norse gods, it is evident that these northern people admired a god who was both wise and brave.

Beneath the third root of Yggdrasil was the sacred well of Urd. From this well, the Norns, or Fates, drew water for the tree. They also mixed water and earth to make a paste which they smeared on the root to protect it from insects, which were constantly attacking it.

The second root was under siege as well, by a dragon who constantly gnawed on it, determined to destroy it.

Another hazard threatened the sacred tree. The Norse believed that as Ragnarok, or doomsday, approached, a great wind would cause Yggdrasil to tremble, signaling its destruction and theirs. The myths of Yggdrasil, as you can see, symbolized a constant struggle between good and evil, and finally, the gloomy prospect of total annihilation.

But as you learned in the previous lesson, the Norse also believed that two human beings would survive Ragnarok, and that Balder the Good would return, marking the beginning of a new and better world.

© 1984, 1997 J. Weston Walch, Publisher   *Mythology: A Teaching Unit*

✎ LET'S SEE WHAT YOU REMEMBER

annihilation   banish   impale   rune   siege

- Let's begin with a little vocabulary quiz. Each of the words above appeared in today's lesson. Your task is to fill in each blank in the sentences that follow with the correct word from the list above.

1. Butterfly collectors used to _____ their specimens on a velvet-covered board and display them prominently.

2. Europe's ancient cities were sometimes enclosed by high walls so that they could withstand a long _____ by their enemies.

3. The threat of atomic warfare is also the threat of total _____ of our world.

4. For displeasing the king, a subject might be _____ (past tense) from the kingdom.

5. Old Norse poetry was sometimes written in _____ (plural).

6. Who was the Greek equivalent of Mimir, the god of wisdom? *Clue:* The owl was her favorite bird. _____

7. From the lesson, you learned that Yggdrasil was an ash tree and that the Druids held the oak sacred. Why do you think these particular trees were chosen? _____

   _____

8. (Optional) The three Norns or Fates were sometimes said to represent past, present, and future. In Charles Dickens's *Christmas Carol*, who were the counterparts of the Norns?

   _____

PART I   LESSON 25

BEOWULF AND KING ARTHUR, TWO NORTHERN HEROES

Beowulf was to the Anglo-Saxon people of England what *The Iliad* and *The Odyssey* were to the Greeks: a wonderfully long poem weaving the exploits of their ancestors with the exploits of mythical characters.

The hero Beowulf, a Geat (Swede), is a noble warrior in the court of King Higlac. Hearing about a horrible monster, Grendel, which has been raiding the palace of Hrothgar, king of the Danes, Beowulf resolves to go to Denmark and do battle with this fearsome creature.

He is graciously received by the elderly Hrothgar, who knew Beowulf's father and who had been a great warrior himself in his youth.

That night, Grendel comes to prey upon the Geats sleeping in the Great Hall of Hrothgar's palace. Beowulf, bare-handed, battles with the monster, succeeds in wrenching its arm from the socket, and sends the beaten and bloody Grendel back to its swampland home.

But Beowulf's trials are not over. Grendel's mother decides to take revenge for her son's mutilation; before Beowulf subdues her, he has a terrible underwater battle from which it hardly seems possible that he will emerge alive.

Having rid Hrothgar's kingdom of the two monsters, Beowulf returns home triumphant, and eventually becomes king of the Geats. In his old age, his kingdom is threatened by a dragon. He slays the dragon to protect his people, but is fatally wounded in the struggle. Still, he dies a hero's death.

◆ ◆ ◆

So far, we have been dealing with myths— stories of ideal heroes. In the King Arthur legend, we meet a real hero. Scholars believe that Arthur was probably a Celtic chieftain who warred against the Saxon invaders of Britain in the fifth century A.D. Recent archeological excavations at Cadbury, in southwest England, show that a huge citadel with twenty-foot-thick walls once existed there. Some historians believe that fortress was actually Camelot.

But the Arthur you may know from the movies *Camelot* and *Excalibur* was a medieval king, quite different from the fifth-century chieftain. For, as his story was told and retold through the centuries, it changed to fit the new ideals of each era. That is the way legends always develop.

Our medieval Arthur was the son of Uther Pendragon, king of Britain. He is brought up as the foster son of Sir Ector, a kindly old knight. Arthur serves as page to Ector's son, Sir Kay.

Merlin, the magician who has watched over Arthur since his birth, acts as tutor to both Kay and Arthur. Thus, he is able to prepare Arthur for kingship without anyone's knowing that Kay's page is actually the king's son.

After Uther Pendragon's death, a tournament is held in London and all the knights attend. In a churchyard there, a sword is embedded in a stone. Whoever can remove it is to be the next king. It is young Arthur who pulls the sword Excalibur from the stone. Then Merlin reveals that the boy is Uther Pendragon's son.

As king, Arthur is determined that his knights will use their might (power) not for selfish gain, but to help the weak who cannot protect themselves. At his famous Round Table, one seat is reserved for the truly pure knight who is destined to succeed in his quest for a vision of the Holy Grail (the cup used by Christ at the Last Supper). Sir Galahad, son of Sir Lancelot and Elaine, eventually has that vision.

Sir Lancelot had come to join Arthur's court earlier, knowing the king's ideals. But he had fallen in love with Arthur's queen, Guinevere. Lancelot and Guinevere's disloyalty to Arthur, combined with the evil Mordred's plotting, eventually destroys Camelot.

In the last great battle, Arthur receives a mortal wound. He then commands Sir Bedivere to return the sword Excalibur to the Lady of the Lake. On a death-barge, Arthur is carried to Avalon (paradise); but the legend closes with a promise that Arthur will return when Britain needs him.

Name _____ Date _____

✎ A NEW CONCEPT OF THE HERO

- Both Beowulf and Arthur are Christian heroes. How do they differ in character from the heroes of ancient Greece? To answer that question, you will need to analyze some of their actions. You are asked to fill in the blanks.

  1. Both Beowulf and Odysseus receive many gifts. Beowulf's come from the grateful king, Hrothgar. Odysseus receives "stranger's gifts." Odysseus hoards his for himself. Beowulf takes them to his king, Higlac. Beowulf is apparently an _____ hero.

  2. Both Beowulf and Odysseus battle monsters. How do their reasons for doing so differ?

     _____

     What characteristic of Beowulf is revealed? _____

  3. Although the hero Odysseus remained firm in his determination to return to his wife, Penelope, he had affairs with both Circe and Calypso during his long journey back to Ithaca. In the King Arthur legend, the highest honor, seeing the Holy Grail, is given to Sir Galahad, the purest of the knights. Lancelot, although he is brave, is a destructive force in Arthur's court because of his relationship with Arthur's wife. What, then, do you see as an important characteristic of the ideal Christian hero?

     _____

     _____

  4. The ancient hero was proud. Remember Achilles sulking in his tent because his commanding general had insulted him by taking his slave girl. Arthur serves as a page to Sir Kay, and even when king, defers to Merlin, who was his tutor. What Christian virtue, one that the ancient hero seldom had, is emphasized in the story of King Arthur?

     _____

     _____

  5. The evil Mordred is often characterized as crafty and always plotting to achieve his objectives. In *The Odyssey*, Athena actually compliments Odysseus for his craftiness. By the medieval period, how do you think the people's attitude toward craftiness had changed?

     _____

     _____

  6. From answers to the preceding questions, plus other ideas you may have formed yourself, state in a sentence how the Christian hero differed from the hero of ancient Greece.

     _____

     _____

     _____

RETA E. KING LIBRARY

✎ TEST I

First, some vocabulary. Match the word with the definition.

WORD	DEFINITION
1. **chronological**	_____ a belief that god is everywhere, in all things
2. **atrophy**	_____ a sudden, unreasoning fear
3. **altruistic**	_____ an abnormal fear of confined places
4. **halcyon**	_____ arranged in the order that events occur
5. **mentor**	_____ to waste or wither away
6. **martial**	_____ calm, tranquil
7. **mercurial**	_____ like Jupiter, majestic
8. **pantheism**	_____ to arouse hope, then disappoint
9. **titan**	_____ a person or thing of great size or power
10. **orgy**	_____ changeable
11. **panic**	_____ warlike
12. **claustrophobia**	_____ wild feasting and celebration
13. **tantalize**	_____ unselfish
14. **Jovian**	_____ a wise and loyal adviser
15. **lethal**	_____ fatal, deadly

• Label each of the following as an allusion (A), a metaphor (M), or a simile (S).

16. _____ Beware of Greeks bearing gifts. (Remember the Trojan Horse.)

17. _____ He worked like a Trojan.

18. _____ He performed a herculean task.

• Now for some symbolism. Complete each sentence appropriately.

19. Midas Muffler Shops' mufflers are gold because _____

_____

20. A publishing house has the owl as its symbol because _____

_____

21. Mobil Oil Corporation uses the flying red horse as its symbol because _____

_____

(continued)

✎ TEST 1 (CONTINUED)

- Here is a chance to characterize the gods. From the list of adjectives in Column B, choose the two that best describe each god or goddess in Column A.

		COLUMN A	COLUMN B	
22. _____ _____		**Zeus**	jealous	gloomy
23. _____ _____		**Poseidon**	warlike	mysterious
24. _____ _____		**Hades**	relentless	fickle
25. _____ _____		**Hera**	beautiful	health-giving
26. _____ _____		**Aphrodite**	reasonable	vain
27. _____ _____		**Athena**	paternal	unfaithful
28. _____ _____		**Artemis**	bloodthirsty	restless
29. _____ _____		**Apollo**	wise	unpredictable
30. _____ _____		**Ares**	just	youthful

- Complete the following statements in the fewest possible words.

31. Prometheus's gift to mankind was important because _____

_____

32. Daphne became a _____

_____

33. Apollo punished Cassandra because she did not keep her _____

_____

34. Zeus sent the great flood because _____

_____

35. The stories of Phaeton and Icarus show that a young person should _____

_____

36. Balder was a kind of _____ figure.

37. Loki represented _____

38. Yggdrasil was guarded by three _____ , or _____

39. Odin so desired knowledge that he was willing to sacrifice one of his _____
    to drink from Mimir's _____

40. At the approach of Ragnarok, the Norse believed Yggdrasil would _____

41. Ragnarok is another name for _____

42. Two natural enemies of Yggdrasil were _____ and a _____ both tried
    to destroy its roots.

SOME SACRED ANIMALS AND GODS OF ANCIENT EGYPT

In Part I, you met the major Greek gods and their Roman counterparts. At this point, you could probably design a family tree showing those gods and goddesses and how they were related to each other.

The gods of Greece and Rome actually were not too numerous. But if you decided to make a family tree for the Egyptian gods, you might get discouraged. They numbered more than a thousand!

Why so many gods? The Egyptian civilization is very ancient. Through the centuries, the names and the characteristics of the gods changed. Sometimes, the characteristics of several earlier gods were consolidated into one later god. Then, too, certain gods were revered in one area, while other gods were worshipped in another area. Also, some gods were animals first who then took on a human appearance. Finally, the myths of Egypt, unlike those of Greece, were handed down orally rather than by written accounts.

But don't be discouraged. You won't encounter all one thousand gods; you will be learning about relatively few, unlike any gods you have already met. The first gods with whom you will become acquainted were half-animal and half-human in form.

Why did the Egyptians give such exalted status to animals? Like other ancient people, they had observed the forces of nature as eternal and unchanging. Thus, they divided their seasons into summer, winter, and inundation—since the Nile overflowed its banks yearly. Animals, too, were unchanging, generation after generation, in character and form. Thus, the Egyptians saw them as eternal as the forces of nature and just as worthy of reverence.

Bulls, cats, hawks, crocodiles, lizards, snakes, and even beetles were among those animals given special status. But cats in general were held in high esteem: They were even embalmed after death and given a coffin burial; and anyone found guilty of killing a cat was apt to receive the death sentence.

Bast, the cat goddess, was portrayed as a woman with the head of a cat. She was the special protectress of pregnant women; but she also protected people from disease and evil spirits. Since she was believed to be fond of music and dancing, her festival was always lively and drew thousands of people.

Taurt, the hippopotamus goddess, also protected women in pregnancy and childbirth. She was depicted as a female hippo standing upright like a human being.

Heket, the frog goddess, was always present at the birth of an Egyptian king since she was associated with both fertility and birth. The people had noticed that frogs were especially plentiful just before the Nile flooded, restoring fertility to the land. Thus, they associated frogs with fertility and new life.

Anubis, the jackal-headed god, was the son of Osiris and Nepthys, who were brother and sister. But Anubis was raised by his aunt Isis, wife and also sister of Osiris. After Osiris's murder, Anubis helped Isis find the scattered parts of her husband's body, reassemble them, and embalm them. This was the beginning of the Egyptian practice of preserving the body. Anubis also guided the dead through the pitfalls of the Underworld to the happy kingdom of Osiris.

One pitfall was Amam, the devourer. When the dead were weighed in judgment, Amam waited by the scales to eat out the heart of anyone who failed the test. With the head and forequarters of a crocodile, the body of a lion, and the hindquarters of a hippopotamus, Amam was fearsome looking.

Benu, a more attractive creature, had the size and form of an eagle, the head of a heron, and plumage of mixed red and gold. He had created himself from fire; thus, the Greeks saw him as a phoenix, and the Egyptians, as a symbol of resurrection.

There were many other gods, of course: Wadjet, the cobra goddess; and Sebek, the crocodile god, for example. But you now have a slight acquaintance with a few of the most interesting ones.

✎ LET'S SEE WHAT YOU REMEMBER

- Answer each question in the space provided, using the fewest possible words.

1. About how many gods did the Egyptians have over the centuries? _____

   _____

2. What was unusual about the early Egyptian gods? (Think of Bast, the cat goddess, and
   Anubis, the jackal-headed god.) _____

   _____

3. How do you account for many different versions of the same story and many different
   names for the same god? _____

   _____

   _____

4. How serious an offense was it to kill a cat? _____

   _____

   _____

5. Scarab bracelets, cut in an oval or beetlelike shape, are still worn. Why do you think they
   might have been popular in Egypt? _____

   _____

   _____

6. What event was foretold by the appearance of large numbers of frogs? _____

   _____

   _____

7. Remember Banu, the exotic bird who had created himself from fire? The Greeks associated
   him with the phoenix, the bird that rose from the ashes. What did the bird actually represent? (Think of fire as a destructive force and of what the bird actually managed to do.)

   _____

   _____

- The following question is not based directly on the lesson, but it asks you to draw a conclusion.

8. Why do you think the Egyptians associated Anubis, the jackal-headed god, with the dead?
   (Think about what the jackal does.) _____

   _____

   _____

PART II **CREATORS AND PROTECTORS** LESSON 28

Like other ancient people, Egyptians speculated on how the world began, and they developed conflicting stories about creation. In the beginning was Nun. Nun was sometimes described as a watery mass from which Ra emerged on the first day and other times depicted as a frog-headed man standing waist deep in water. From his body, the gods emerged, earning him the title of father of the gods. Both stories have in common with the creation myths of many lands the belief that life came originally from the water.

Hap, god of the Nile, is generally regarded as the father of human beings. In one myth, humans were created from his tears. Coming later than Nun, Hap assumed some of the older god's attributes.

In another imaginative story, Geb was the creator and, like Nun, was the father of the gods. Geb was also the god of the earth's surface, and his sister and wife, Nut, was goddess of the sky. In another version, Nut was the wife of Ra, the sun god, who tried to keep her apart from Geb and who condemned her to being barren. Nevertheless, Nut and Geb produced Osiris, Isis, Set, Nephthys, and Horus.

Geb and Nut's relationship was unconventional, but not unusual among the gods. What is unusual in the myth is that earth (Geb) was masculine. Generally, earth is the female force and sky is the male force. What is more, it was Geb who laid the egg from which the world emerged.

Another being worth knowing was Bes, the dwarf god. You may remember lame Hephaestus, the only Greek god not perfect in form, who was scorned by the others. Bes fared better and was important to the Egyptians because he brought good luck, protected women during childbirth,

and was the patron of art and music. Bes was the god of war as well.

Two of Geb's children, a brother and sister who married each other, were well known and admired by the Egyptians. They were Osiris and Isis, whose love story has elements of tragedy. Osiris had been a good king, teaching his people agricultural methods, giving them religious instruction, and codifying their laws. But his jealous brother, Set, plotted Osiris's assassination and accomplished it by nailing him into a coffinlike box and throwing the box into the Nile.

Isis eventually recovered her husband's body and brought it back to Egypt. But evil Set discovered it, cut it into pieces, and then scattered the pieces. Once more, Isis searched for and found her husband's remains and, with the help of Anubis, reassembled them. Osiris was eventually resurrected and reigns in the kingdom of the dead. For the people, he came to represent the past, present, and future. He gave them the hope that as his followers, they, too, could achieve immortality.

Set continued to harass Isis. He was determined to destroy her son Horus. But Isis managed to hide the boy from him. Eventually, Horus engaged Set in battle and emerged victorious, thus avenging his father's murder.

Isis came to be admired even outside Egypt. The Greeks and Romans actually built temples in her honor. Among early Christians, her attributes became those of the Virgin Mary. Her wanderings with Horus seemed to parallel Mary's wanderings with the Christ child.

As for the Egyptians themselves, they believed Isis's tears for Osiris caused the Nile to overflow its banks yearly, reviving the fertility of the land. Isis was their goddess of the harvest, their, queen of the underworld, and their most important goddess.

© 1984, 1997 J. Weston Walch, Publisher   *Mythology: A Teaching Unit*

PART II   WORKSHEET 28

✎ THE GODS ON TRIAL

- Imagine that you are a court reporter, trying to get a scoop for your newspaper. You attend each of the following trials. A summary of the case is provided, but you must identify the plaintiff, defendant, or other god mentioned in each summary. Fill in the blanks.

  1. A. _____ demands reparation from B. _____ for stealing the affection of A.'s wife and leading her into adultery. Plaintiff A. states that there can be no doubt that adultery occurred since the two guilty parties have produced five children.

  2. A. _____ demands that B. _____ be prosecuted to the full extent of the law for the heinous crime of murdering and dismembering her husband.

  3. A. _____ accuses B. _____ of harassing her and threatening her young son C. _____ .

- As a reporter, you need a good vocabulary. Can you define each of the following words from the sentences above? Write your own definition first. Then verify it by checking the word in a dictionary.

  4. **reparation** _____

  5. **heinous** _____

  6. **harassment** _____

  7. **plaintiff** _____

  8. **prosecute** _____

OPTIONAL QUESTION

  9. In Christian belief, reference to the Holy Family actually means Mary, Joseph, and Jesus. Who were their equivalents in Egyptian mythology?

     _____

THE EGYPTIAN VIEW OF DEATH AND THE AFTERLIFE

Have you ever played word associations? For example, if someone says "rose," you are supposed to answer with whatever word comes to mind first. Would it be "red" or "flower" or "thorn"? (Actually, most people say "red.") Now suppose someone in the game says "Egypt." What would you think of first? Nile River? Sphinx? pyramids?

If you have ever seen a mummy in the Egyptian section of a museum, you would probably think of that experience first. It is not one you could easily forget. The skin probably looked so dark, dry, and leathery that it was difficult for you to imagine the mummy as a person much like yourself, although thousands of years older.

Perhaps you wonder how the Egyptians were able to preserve the bodies of the dead or, more important, why they preserved them. To answer the first question, they used certain substances that protected the corpse from decay and used extensive wrappings to shut out the air. Elaborate rituals were also part of the embalming process, rituals that seemed to have magical results.

As for why the bodies were preserved, you must remember that the Egyptian view of life after death was quite different from ours. The Egyptians believed that the soul and body would eventually be reunited and that the individual would resume a lifestyle not too different from what it had been on earth. That is why—if the person had been wealthy enough—food, clothing, weapons, and even furniture were all placed in the tomb with the body.

Egyptian kings were buried in rich garments. Their jewels and other valuables were put in the tomb as well. And, of course, their tombs were very splendid; they were the pyramids, large enough to contain everything the ruler might need in the next world.

The Egyptians had a name for the soul: Ba. Ba was generally depicted as a hawk with a man's head. When someone died, the belief was that Ba entered the tomb to visit the body from which it had temporarily been separated. So firm was this belief that a small opening was always left in the tomb for Ba to enter; and inside, a perch was provided for him.

Tuat, the Underworld, was not actually beneath the ground. It was located in the sky, separated from the gods' dwelling by a mountain range and from the earth by more mountains. It was a long, mysterious valley divided by a river, along which lurked devils and fierce beasts, all ready to prey upon the dead.

To elude these would-be destroyers, recently deceased people used a variety of spells, incantations, and prayers from the *Book of the Dead*. If they successfully avoided the perils along the way, they reached the kingdom of Osiris, a place of perpetual joy and happiness.

With such a pleasant prospect in store, death itself may not have seemed such a frightening experience. If the Egyptians needed any further convincing, they had the example of Osiris himself; he, too, had once been a mortal. Despite being murdered and dismembered, he had been resurrected to reign forever in the kingdom of the dead.

✎ MAPPING THE UNDERWORLD

- Your assignment is to draw a map of Tuat, the Underworld, making certain to include all the features listed below.

  1. Locate Tuat geographically, showing its position in relation to the dwelling place of the gods and to earth.

  2. Include any significant natural features such as rivers and mountains.

  3. Show Tuat's regular inhabitants. Use stick figures if necessary, and place them where a traveler would be most apt to encounter them.

  4. Include warning signs for travelers, pointing out perils they might have to deal with from the moment they enter the Underworld. Don't forget Amam.

  5. Most travelers carry a map or guidebook. What special guidebook will you recommend to these poor souls? Write its title on your map, near the starting point of the journey.

  6. Don't forget to show the travelers' final destination.

THINKING IT OVER

  7. The obstacles or perils the dead people had to overcome to reach eternal happiness might, symbolically, mean that they had to atone for sin before they were resurrected in a kind of paradise. Is there any equivalent experience in Christian belief? Explain.

_____

_____

_____

_____

CHINESE CREATION MYTHS

As you learned from studying Egyptian mythology, ancient civilizations accumulated numerous myths, and individual storytellers created their own versions of the old tales. China, being of great antiquity, probably has a larger store of literature than any other civilization; and since many Chinese myths were collected long after their period of origin, seemingly conflicting versions of the same story exist.

This is true of the creation myths. In one, dating possibly to the third century B.C., Hu was the emperor of the Northern Sea and his counterpart Shu, was emperor of the Southern Sea. Halfway between their kingdoms was the territory of Hundun, emperor of the center, whose name meant chaos.

Hundun, unfortunately, had no orifices for seeing, hearing, breathing, or eating. To help him, Hu and Shu bored holes in him, one each day, until on the seventh day, Hundun died. From the holes his friends bored, the world emerged. Thus Hundun, the creator, died to produce the world.

In an earlier story, P'an Ku was the creator. He was a man, not a god, born of an egg that separated into two parts: heaven and earth. The heavy part (earth) became yin, and the light part (sky) became yang.

For the next 18,000 years, the distance between heaven and earth grew at the rate of ten feet a day. P'an Ku grew at the same rate to fill the void between them. At the end of that time, he died. From his body parts emerged the features of the universe: mountain ranges from his head, stomach, arms, and feet; the sun and moon from his eyes; plants, stars, and planets from his hair; metal and stones from his teeth and bones; jade from his bone marrow; and pearls from his

semen. As for human beings, they were created from the fleas on his body.

In another myth, the goddess Nugua created men and women. At first, she modeled them carefully from clay; but soon she became impatient with the process. So she took a rope and dragged it through mud. The drops that fell off the rope became peasants while the modeled figures became aristocrats.

In yet another story, P'an Ku tried to make people from clay and to endow them with yin or yang (female or male life force). When a storm came up suddenly, he hastily gathered up the figures, marring some in the process. The damaged ones became deformed people.

While the P'an Ku creation myth has yang and yin as parts of the egg from which he emerged, in other accounts, yang and yin are the parents of all creatures, of all natural geographic features, of the stars, and even of the seasons. This theory is in keeping with the beliefs of one of China's great religions, Taoism, which holds that there is a universal energy that is the basis of everything in nature. In this system, yang and yin—positive and negative, male and female, light and darkness, heat and cold—balance each other and make creation possible.

By now, you are probably aware that many creation myths have certain features in common: the selfless person or god whose sacrifice or death makes life possible for others; the state of chaos before some force brings order to the world or universe; and the egg as a symbol for the beginning or the emergence of life as we know it. As you look at other stories of creation, try to determine if their underlying concepts are ones you have encountered before.

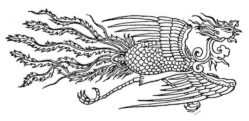

✎ READING BETWEEN THE LINES

- Answer the following in the fewest possible words.

1. In the myth of Hu, Shu, and Hundun, why was it inevitable that Hundun die in order for the world to emerge? (Think of what the name Hundun actually means.)

   _____

   _____

   _____

2. In the two stories of creation of human beings—from the fleas on P'an Ku's body, and from the mud droplets on Nugua's rope—what attitude toward individuals of the human species

   seems to be expressed? _____

   _____

   _____

   Do you think the individual was important? Explains _____

   _____

   _____

   _____

3. What did Hundun and P'an Ku have in common? (Think of their greatest

   contribution.) _____

   _____

   _____

4. Without referring to the lesson, list the properties of yin and yang.

   YIN   YANG

   _____   _____

   _____   _____

   _____   _____

   _____   _____

   _____   _____

PART II **ANIMALS IN CHINESE MYTHOLOGY** LESSON 31

Remember Beowulf (Lesson 25), who as a young warrior wrestled with and killed Grendel and Grendel's mother? In old age, Beowulf, by then the king of Sweden, fought and killed a dragon who was terrorizing his people. In the struggle, Beowulf received a mortal wound as well.

In Western literature such as *Beowulf,* dragons were depicted as destructive and death dealing. In the Chinese myths, they played a different role. They were considered useful and beneficial creatures, responsible for such tasks as guarding the mansions of the gods and protecting hidden treasure from would-be thieves. Because they controlled the wind and rain, dragons benefited farmers. They were also capable of clearing streams and deepening the seas—engineering feats that benefited everyone.

The dragon was a symbol of spring; thus, its color was green. It represented yang, the positive male force. The dragon was so admired by the Chinese that they frequently depicted it in their art. In fact, they still do.

Another mythical animal, the unicorn, is probably already familiar to you. In recent years, it has appeared on T-shirts, greeting cards, and posters. It seems to be enjoying a renaissance. In appearance, it is a cross between a deer and a horse, with a large horn protruding from its forehead—its most distinctive feature.

Despite its gentle appearance, the the unicorn of Chinese legend was capable of using its horn as a lethal weapon in combat against evil. In these animals, the Chinese saw strength and virtue combined—both the yang and the yin.

Later, in the medieval period, the unicorn was actually hunted, but it remained elusive. In one tale, however, hunters tricked it, using a beautiful maiden as a decoy. The unicorn saw the maiden and was attracted by her apparent innocence and purity. He rested his head on her lap and went to sleep. The maiden then summoned the hunters to capture the unicorn.

Like the Egyptians and other ancients, the Chinese revered the red bird, or phoenix—a bird of prey, eaglelike in appearance. The bird symbolized fire, since it seemed able to regenerate or resurrect itself from the ashes. In another version of this myth, the young bird emerged from the dead body of its parent. Thus, although the bird was associated with resurrection, it was also associated with death. To the Chinese, the phoenix embodied the female force, yin. Its season was summer.

The creature whose season was autumn was for the Chinese the king of the beasts. He was not the lion, but the white tiger—an animal both respected and feared. Any human being eaten by a tiger fell under the animal's power and, in turn, preyed like a tiger on other humans.

The tortoise represented winter. A slow-moving and somewhat withdrawn creature, it was credited with very special powers. Supposedly, it knew the secrets of life and death.

Certain domestic animals earned the gratitude of the Chinese. The dog was credited with introducing them to their staple food, rice. The ox, it was said, had come down from heaven to urge people to work hard so that they would have food to eat. The ox also helped them with the plowing to make certain that they had abundant crops.

By now, you must realize that although the Chinese attitude toward animals differed from the Egyptian, both civiliations saw animals as important inhabitants of their world.

Name _____ Date _____

✎ BEASTS, REAL AND IMAGINARY

- Without reviewing the lesson, see how well you can match the characteristics in Column I with the beasts in Column II

<table>
<tr><td colspan="2" align="center">COLUMN I
CHARACTERISTICS</td><td align="center">COLUMN II
ANIMALS</td></tr>
<tr><td>1. _____</td><td>knew the secrets of life and death</td><td>A. dragon</td></tr>
<tr><td>2. _____</td><td>appreciated purity and innocence</td><td></td></tr>
<tr><td>3. _____</td><td>was able to regenerate itself</td><td></td></tr>
<tr><td>4. _____</td><td>had one remarkable weapon of defense</td><td>B. tortoise</td></tr>
<tr><td>5. _____</td><td>occasionally ate a person</td><td></td></tr>
<tr><td>6. _____</td><td>represented winter</td><td></td></tr>
<tr><td>7. _____</td><td>was a bird of prey</td><td>C. unicorn</td></tr>
<tr><td>8. _____</td><td>had a balance of yang and yin within itself</td><td></td></tr>
<tr><td>9. _____</td><td>was a good civil engineer</td><td>D. dog</td></tr>
<tr><td>10. _____</td><td>controlled the wind and rain</td><td></td></tr>
<tr><td>11. _____</td><td>represented spring</td><td></td></tr>
<tr><td>12. _____</td><td>was feared in other societies</td><td>E. ox</td></tr>
<tr><td>13. _____</td><td>guarded treasure</td><td></td></tr>
<tr><td>14. _____</td><td>encouraged humans to work</td><td></td></tr>
<tr><td>15. _____</td><td>gave human beings the gift of rice</td><td>F. phoenix</td></tr>
</table>

MYTHS IN TODAY'S WORLD

16. What two mythlike creatures apparently inhabit today's world, since sightings of them are frequently reported in the newspapers?

_____

_____

_____

_____

PART II GODS AND ANCESTORS LESSON 32

You are about to meet just a few of the many Chinese gods. First, among the immortals living on the sacred mountain of Tai Shan was the supreme god Jade Yudi. It was to this heavenly emperor that his mortal counterpart made sacrifices. In some myths, Jade Yudi was the creator of human beings, fashioning them from clay. In a sudden storm, some of his newly made figures got wet. Those unfortunates began life with some physical handicap or were prone to illness. Does that story sound familiar? You read of it in another myth.

Outstanding among the immortals was Kuan Yin, goddess of mercy. (Actually, she was imported from India, where she had been a Buddhist deity with a different name.) Kuan Yin was the bringer of children and the mother goddess. In this capacity, she is said to have watered the rice plants with her own milk so that they would flourish.

An interesting trio were the three gods of happiness. All had been mortals before being transformed into gods. First was Shoulao, god of long life; present at births, he made an immediate decision as to how long a life the newborn would have. The second member of the trio was Luxing, god of salaries. The third of these deified humans was Fuxing, whose title actually was god of happiness.

The Chinese strove not only to retain the goodwill of these and many other gods but also to please the ancestors, who exerted quite an influence on the living. People engaged in elaborate rituals to the dead, but these did not always succeed. Sometimes they couldn't even get through to the deceased. Even when they did, they couldn't be certain that the spirits would be in a frame of mind to answer their questions.

Actually, only the king and his court attempted these séances. Ordinary people who wanted to know about the future had to rely on sorcerers. The ruler alone had the authority to query his ancestors or the gods about receiving boons, such as good harvests or success in battle. This privilege put him in a rather precarious position, however. For if natural phenomena such as droughts or earthquakes occurred, the people saw them as indications that the ruler's relationship with the immortals was strained and therefore questioned whether he was ideally suited to his role.

As for the actual method of contact, it was by divination—using omens to foretell the future. A question would be asked, and the answer would be found by reading the cracks on scorched bones of animals or tortoise shells. Since questions and answers were usually recorded, we know that queries about the gender of an unborn child were popular. The answer was good if it was to be a boy and not good if a girl was on the way.

As an indication of their respect for the dead, the Chinese attempted to embalm the corpses. But they were not as successful as the Egyptians, except with those bodies that were placed in certain caves with atmospheric conditions just right for preservation.

Kings were buried with great pomp. Human sacrifices were made so that the king would not meet death alone. He was sent to the Other World with goods such as brass cauldrons, weapons, jewels, and whatever else he would need in the future. Such elaborate preparations for burial indicate that the Chinese had no doubt that there was life after death.

✎ WORDS IN CONTEXT AND A FEW THOUGHT QUESTIONS

- Let's start with some vocabulary from the lesson. When you saw each of the following words in context, what did you think it meant? Write your definition first. Then use a dictionary to verify it.

    1. **capacity** _____

    2. **deified** _____

    3. **séance** _____

    4. **sorcerer** _____

    5. **precarious** _____

    6. **pomp** _____

    7. **cauldron** _____

- In the following questions, you are asked to make some judgments.

    8. What sets Kuan Yin apart from the other gods and goddesses you have met?

    _____

    _____

    _____

    9. In addition to Luxing, god of salaries, the Chinese had another deity, Zai Shen, who was god of wealth. Does that information give you a clue as to what they considered important?

    _____

    _____

    _____

    10. What do you think the Chinese attitude toward females was? Explain.

    _____

    _____

    _____

BONUS QUESTION

    11. A practice still in existence is the "reading" of tea leaves. A fortune-teller examines the tea leaves in the bottom of the teacup and foretells the future based on the pattern formed by the leaves. In this lesson, what new word did you learn that would describe the process the

    fortune-teller uses? _____

PART II

THE WORLD'S CYCLE OF DEATH AND REBIRTH

Living in a country to which European settlers came scarcely four hundred years ago, we may have difficulty imagining the continuity of ancient civilizations—where the same rituals and customs have been part of the culture for not just hundreds but thousands of years.

In our country, the European settlers found Native Americans, whose way of life was far different from their own. Gradually the settlers accepted some of the Native American ways. The process continues. Only recently have we begun to see the true wisdom of the Native Americans' reverence for the land and belief that it is held only in trust from the Great Spirit. In the same way, the ancient civilizations of Egypt, China, and India gradually accepted and modified new customs, new rituals, and new religious beliefs and made them part of their lives.

Nowhere was this process of assimilation more active than in India. Thus, Indian myths are varied and in some ways unique. But as in every other mythology we have studied, the Indian stories try to provide answers about how the universe began and how the human race came into existence. And, as always, there is the question about who or what set everything in motion.

Before going further, you need to know something about the framework of Hindu thought. Hindus believe that everything good or evil is a manifestation of the Universal Spirit, Iswara. All things are part of a cycle of creation that goes on forever: The world as we know it is destroyed, and the world is re-created. Because this cycle takes so many millions of years, it is hard to grasp the pattern. Three gods, or manifestations of the Universal Spirit, accomplish each cycle by performing specific tasks: Brahma creates, Vishnu preserves, and Siva destroys.

Let's try to put their activities into a time frame. Whenever Brahma wakes up, the world and all its creatures come into being. Since a single day in his life equals 43,200,000 years, the world will exist for a very long time before becoming part of the Universal Spirit once more.

Brahma, of course, does not work alone. Vishnu, the preserver and protector, comes to earth whenever there seems to be danger of its being destroyed prematurely—as when some evil power attempts to take over. When a great flood was imminent, Vishnu appeared to a wise man as a fish and advised him to build a boat. Other guises assumed by Vishnu when visiting earth include a tortoise, a bear, and a man-lion.

Siva's task is the ultimate destruction of the old, worn-out world. (Do you see that Siva is actually death?) Siva is also the god of the dance; as the world nears its end, Siva dances until the world is reabsorbed into the Universal Spirit. Siva is an ascetic (one who practices self-denial, avoiding physical pleasure and engaging in spiritual activities). But several beautiful women have been attracted to him. The first, Sati, loved him dearly, and he grew to love her, too. But she committed suicide by throwing herself into a bonfire. Siva immediately began a dance of mourning, which soon turned into the dance of destruction. That dance would have destroyed the world prematurely if Vishnu, the preserver, had not intervened.

Now you have met the principal actors in this drama of death and rebirth. In the next lesson, you will read the colorful and poetic story of the beginning of existence.

© 1984, 1997 J. Weston Walch, Publisher

Mythology: A Teaching Unit

PART II   ✎ WORDS AND THOUGHTS   WORKSHEET 33

ascetic   assimilation   custom   manifestation   prematurely   ritual

_____   _____   _____   _____   _____   _____

- All of these words appeared in today's lesson. Go back to the lesson to see them in context. Then write what you think is the meaning of each word on the line just below it. Then, referring to your list of meanings as a guide, complete each of the following sentences, using the appropriate word in its appropriate form.

1. Because the baby was born _____ , it was underweight at birth.

2. In their freshman year at college, many students have difficulty _____ the many new ideas being presented to them.

3. At weddings, it is a time-honored _____ to throw rice at the bride and groom as they come out of the church.

4. A wedding is one of the great _____ (plural) of a person's life.

5. The saintly hermit led an _____ life, eating only enough to sustain himself, dressing simply, avoiding any occasion for sin, and devoting himself to meditation.

6. Mrs. Barrington-Jones attended a séance, hoping she would be able to contact the Spirit World and see some _____ that would prove her dead husband was trying to reach out to her from beyond the grave.

THINKING IT OVER

7. Siva was called the destroyer—not a title that many people would want. But was his work necessary? Explain. _____

_____

8. If the whole world is re-created each time Brahma awakes, then it follows that people are re-created or reincarnated, too. How does this automatic reincarnation differ from the Egyptian idea that the soul and body would eventually be reunited and the dead would reach Osiris's kingdom? Explain. _____

_____

9. You may have heard people say, "Next time around, I'd like to be a dog; after all, a dog's life is pretty easy" or, "If you could be any animal, which one would you be?" What are they really talking about? _____

10. What is your understanding of the term Universal Spirit? _____

_____

_____

In the previous lesson, you were introduced to the Hindu concept of the world's being destroyed and re-created as Brahma sleeps and wakes. Remember that the process is a very slow one, since Brahma's day lasts more than 43 million years.

In the period of the nonexistence—when Brahma sleeps and world is reabsorbed into the Universal Spirit—the world is represented as Vishnu lying on a thousand-headed cobra (a symbol of eternity) and floating in an ocean of milk.

Eventually a lotus appears out of Vishnu's navel. Seated on the lotus is Brahma, who has returned to begin his task of re-creation.

In another myth, Purusha creates the world. A manifestation of the Universal Spirit, Purusha emerges from a giant golden egg, serenely floating on the water. Like the cobra in the other myth, Purusha has a thousand limbs, a thousand heads, a thousand faces, and a thousand eyes—one per head.

Purusha sacrifices himself so that the universe can come into existence. Then creatures begin emerging from his body, according to a caste system. Gods and the followers of Brahma come from his mouth, merchants and cattle emerge from his thighs, laborers and horses come from his feet, and demons come from his abdomen. Thus, both good and evil are accounted for. The obvious parallel here is the P'an Ku creation myth; but remember, the features of the universe emerged from P'an Ku, while human beings were created from the fleas on his body.

For the ordinary person, the idea of reincarnation each time the new world emerged might have been a comforting concept—it offered a chance of immortality. But for certain ascetic scholars, the wheel, or cycle of life, death, and rebirth, seemed burdensome—something from which they wanted to escape. These scholars believed that if they could purge themselves of all desire and emotion, which cause people's sorrows and joys, they could circumvent that endless cycle and remain in a blissful state of nonexistence.

This was the viewpoint offered by Buddha, who lived several centuries before the time of Christ. He taught that to eliminate desire was to eliminate suffering as well. Each person should practice self-denial and show compassion for others. By following the Buddhist eightfold path, a set of rules for ethical conduct, the person could hope to reach Nirvana (blissful nonexistence). Remember that Kuan Yin, the Chinese goddess of mercy and compassion, had her origin in Indian Buddhism.

In Indian mythology, Buddha eventually came to be regarded as one of the incarnations of Vishnu, a good example of the Indians' assimilation of new concepts into their existing mythology.

✎ HOW GOOD IS YOUR RECALL?

- Let's try a matching game to see how well you remember the details of this lesson. Match the name in Column A with the description in Column B. *Note:* The lists do not match evenly.

COLUMN A	COLUMN B
1. _____ **Nirvana**	A. lived several centuries before Christ, taught the eightfold path, emphasized self-denial and compassion for others.
2. _____ **Purusha**	B. the preserver, appeared in many forms
3. _____ **Vishnu**	C. Brahma sat here.
4. _____ **Buddha**	D. Purusha emerged from it.
5. _____ **Kuan Yin**	E. goddess of mercy
6. _____ **Brahma**	F. held up Vishnu
7. _____ **the cobra**	G. the source of all things
8. _____ **the cosmic egg**	H. the state of blissful nonexistence
9. _____ **Universal Spirit**	I. creator of humans and animals
10. _____ **the Lotus**	J. When he awakes, the world reemerges.
	K. Buddha became one of his incarnations.

🖎 **TEST II**

- For the first fifteen questions, match the god or goddess in Column I with the description in Column II.

COLUMN I	COLUMN II

1. **Anubis**

2. **Osiris**

3. **Isis**

4. **Ra**

5. **Geb**

6. **Hundun**

7. **Kuan Yin**

8. **Nugua**

9. **Bast**

10. **Jade yudi**

11. **P'an Ku**

12. **Siva**

13. **Set**

14. **Brahma**

15. **Vishnu**

A. _____ She was a loving wife and an important goddess in her own right.

B. _____ From his body, all living things were created. He lived 18,000 years.

C. _____ The sun god whose wife was unfaithful.

D. _____ He was the first to perform an embalming.

E. _____ He represented earth.

F. _____ She was the goddess of mercy.

G. _____ Because she liked song and dance, her festivals were lively.

H. _____ He died, was resurrected, and reigns in the kingdom of the dead.

I. _____ He was supreme ruler among the gods.

J. _____ She began fashioning humans from clay, but soon got bored.

K. _____ He was the destroyer.

L. _____ He had no orifices with which to eat, hear, or see.

M. _____ As he sleeps and wakes, the world is destroyed and reconstructed.

N. _____ He was the evil brother and uncle.

O. _____ He was the preserver.

- The following names are actually symbolic and based on myths you have read. Complete each sentence.

16. An insurance company is named Phoenix Fire Insurance because

_____

_____

17. A stock mutual fund with investments in China is called Colonial Newport Tiger
Fund because _____

_____

_____

✎ TEST II (CONTINUED)

- Now let's try some vocabulary from the lessons. For sentences 18 through 25, fill in each blank with one of the following words.

   orifice   pomp   heinous   manifestation   attribute

18. When Queen Elizabeth addresses the British parliament, it is an occasion

    of great _____ . She rides through the streets of London in her royal coach.

19. A ghost is a _____ from the spirit world.

20. The mouth is one of the body's _____ (plural). The nose is another.

21. The Lizzie Borden axe murder was considered a _____ crime.

22. Over the centuries, the _____ (plural) of one god were sometimes given to
    another.

- Complete the following sentences, using the fewest possible words.

   23. The Egyptian gods were interesting and unusual because they were often, in part,

       _____ .

   24. Two symbols of the source of all life which appear often in the myths are _____
       and the _____.

   25. To create the world, the creator often gave up his _____ .

BONUS QUESTION

   26. Osiris's death and resurrection could be compared with what religious figure and event in
       Christian belief ?

       _____

       _____

PART III AFRICAN ANIMALS AND GODS   LESSON 36

From recent discoveries of fossilized human bones in Africa, scientists estimate that human life there dates back more than four million years. Unfortunately, not much early history exists of African people who lived south of the Sahara Desert. Also, unlike other ancient cultures, Africa developed no unified collection of myths.

From social studies, you know that Africa is a vast continent with natural barriers—mountains and deserts—that isolated one group of people from another. The fact that several different languages were spoken set up a cultural barrier as well. Thus, it is understandable that a variety of myths existed.

Myths of the Northeast, now Sudan and Ethiopia, showed similarities to those of the Egyptians. Animal gods were worshiped (even a hippopotamus goddess like the Egyptian Tuart), and they were succeeded by half-human, half-animal gods.

People wore animal masks, believing that in doing so, they acquired the animal's strength, and the animal became their protector. Like the Egyptian cats, some animals were given high status. Snakes, the symbol of royalty, were also supposed to possess special powers. In a myth from Ghana, a python's ritual and spell brought children to a couple who had previously been childless. Ever after, as a mark or respect, pythons were given proper burial. For yet another reason, snakes were respected—it was always possible that the snake was one's ancestor, for the dead could return to earth as snakes or leopards or lions.

The hyena, not an especially attractive beast, nevertheless had special skills. He was a wizard who could change at will from animal to human form. He also had earned a reputation as a sly trickster. In one myth, the hyena and the hare, in a time of famine, agreed to kill their mothers for food. (Cannibalism was actually practiced in some areas.) The hyena did kill his mother, but the hare went back on his word. Angered, the hyena killed the hare's mother anyway. But in this myth it is the hare who is the trickster, eventually killing the hyena and a lion as well.

The hyena and the hare came to this country; only their names were changed. African slaves, imported to work on the plantations of the South, brought their myths with them. The hyena became Brer Fox and the hare, Brer Rabbit.

Sierra Leone and Ghana in West Africa contributed the myth of the spider Anansi, another trickster, and a ruthless one at that. Anansi wanted to buy stories from a sky god, renowned as a storyteller. The god set a high price. Anansi had to bring him a python, a hornet, and a nature spirit. Anansi agreed to the terms and offered his mother as a bonus. By trickery, he was able to collect everyone the god had requested and brought them, along with his mother, to the great storyteller. The god kept his part of the bargain and turned his stories over to Anansi.

In contrast to Anansi was Yiyi, another spider, who was credited with stealing fire from the sky and bringing it to mankind. You might say that Yiyi was the Prometheus of the animal kingdom.

Although Anansi managed to capture a nature spirit, people generally feared them and feared their own ancestral spirits as well. Gods and spirits were everywhere. Sun, moon, earth, forests, rivers, even the ocean were divinities whom people dared not offend. Dwarf demons lurked in the forest and delighted in devouring human flesh. The Abatwa, people so small that they slept in anthills, amused themselves by shooting arrows at passersby. Given all these potential dangers, life must have been perilous indeed.

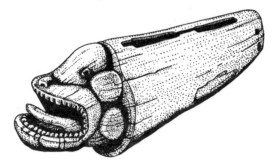

✎ RITUALS AND REFLECTIONS

- Let's begin with a few vocabulary words. In Lesson 32, you learned that the Chinese used divination. If you don't remember exactly what divination is, check the dictionary and write down the definition. _____

  _____

  African people used divination as well, but they had some other interesting practices that you did not encounter in the mythologies you have already studied. These were fetishism and totemism. Read the definitions below carefully; then try to answer the questions that follow.

    A. **Fetishism**—showing reverence for some object believed to have magical powers.
    B. **Totemism**—believing that some natural object such as a plant or animal has a blood relationship through heredity to a particular family or tribe.

1. Have you ever carried a rabbit's foot? If so, why did you do it?

   _____

2. Is carrying a rabbit's foot and believing in its power an example of A or B? _____

3. Have you ever heard of worry stones? _____

   _____

4. What special property are they supposed to have? _____

   _____

5. Have you ever heard about totems before? If so, in what connection? _____

   _____

6. Do you know where in this country you might find totems?

   _____

- Let's reflect a little on the stories in today's lesson.

7. In the one about the hyena and the hare, what justification was given for their decision to kill their mothers? _____

   _____

8. If you have ever heard the term "survival of the fittest," what is your understanding of its meaning? _____

   _____

9. Can you apply the term to this myth? Explain briefly. _____

   _____

10. What one adjective would you use to describe Anansi the spider? (Don't use an adjective that appeared in the lesson.)

    _____

PART III   TWO AFRICAN TALES   LESSON 37

On his long journey home to Ithaca after the Trojan War, the Greek hero Odysseus faced many dangers but was clever enough to get himself out of tight spots. In fact, the goddess Athena called him "Never At a Loss," because she so admired his ingenuity.

A Ghana myth describes another hero's exploits. He was Number Eleven, so named because he was the youngest of eleven children. Their mother was like the Old Woman in the Shoe, for her children had such voracious appetites that they ate all the food. As a consequence, she was starving to death and didn't know what to do.

Knowing that the children were going to a certain pumpkin patch to gather food, she asked a tree that overhung the patch to drop its branches on them and kill them all—a pretty drastic solution! But Number Eleven thwarted her plan, and they harvested and ate the pumpkins.

The Sky God was her next ally in her attempt to rid herself of her children. Number Eleven bested him several times. Finally, in exasperation, the Sky God sent the children on a quest for four golden objects obtainable only in the village of Death. Number Eleven had his work cut out for him this time, for Death intended to eat the children, but he tricked her, too, and obtained the golden objects the Sky God had described.

Death did not give up easily, but after several more encounters with Number Eleven, she acknowledged that she was beaten and promised not to bother him again.

If you have read Shakespeare's *Romeo and Juliet*, you know that Juliet refuses to marry the man her father has chosen for her and that she falls in love with Romeo at first sight and secretly marries him. Although the love story ends tragically, the families of Romeo and Juliet agree to stop feuding—so the play ends on a positive note.

An African myth from Nigeria has some similarities to the Romeo-Juliet story. A beautiful girl, Nkoyo, spurns each suitor her father chooses for her. Meanwhile, a skull from the Bush of the Ghosts decides to woo her. Wisely, he first borrows the finest of body parts from each of his friends so that he can appear before her in a very attractive form.

When he arrives in Nkoyo's village and she sees him, like Juliet, she falls wildly in love. Her parents are troubled because they know nothing about the man, but finally they agree to the marriage. Immediately after the ceremony, the skull wants to take his bride back to his own country. The poor father, sad to lose his beautiful daughter, nevertheless cautions her to be obedient to her new husband.

As they travel toward the skull's home, he returns each body part to its rightful owner, and the poor bride is left finally with only a skull for a husband. In addition, she now has the task of caring for his old mother. But Nkoyo remembers her father's words and becomes a model wife.

The story has a happy ending, for the old mother-in-law saves the girl when the other people in the Bush of Ghosts are plotting to kill her. She returns to her own home and marries the man her father had chosen for her.

✎ WORDS AND MEANINGS

- Have you ever tried the *Reader's Digest* quiz "It Pays to Increase Your Word Power"? If you have, you know that twenty words are listed with multiple choice definitions. As a reader, you are asked to select the correct definition.

  Let's see how well you can do in choosing the correct definition for each of the following words. All of them appeared in today's lesson. You will probably want to read the stories again and see the words in context before you try the quiz.

1. _____   **ally** (noun)   (a) a narrow corridor between two buildings   (b) a glass marble   (c) someone you can count on to help you   (d) one who is on the opposite team

2. _____   **drastic** (adjective)   (a) harsh, apt to burn the skin   (b) flexible   (c) outstanding, (d) extreme in effect

3. _____   **exasperation** (noun)   (a) annoyance   (b) breathing out   (c) state of confusion (d) aggressiveness

4. _____   **ingenuity** (noun)   (a) lacking in genius   (b) resourcefulness (c) belonging to a particular family   (d) innocence

5. _____   **spurn** (verb)   (a) stir up (as a fire)   (b) turn on a spindle   (c) seek out, (d) reject distainfully

6. _____   **thwart** (verb)   (a) threaten   (b) taunt or insult   (c) prevent or defeat (d) abolish

7. _____   **voracious** (adjective)   (a) highly motivated   (b) difficult to, satisfy (c) uncontrolled   (d) puzzled

8. In one sense, both the stories have to do with resurrection. Can you explain how? *Clue:* Think of the places Number Eleven and Nkoyo visited. _____

   _____

   _____

9. The story of Nkoyo has a moral. What is it? _____

   _____

   _____

10. In an earlier lesson, you were asked to define "survival of the fittest." In the story of Number Eleven, how is it demonstrated by his brothers and mother? _____

   _____

   _____

WHEN OUR LAND WAS YOUNG— NATIVE AMERICAN MYTHS

Nineteenth-century poet Henry Wadsworth Longfellow wrote a long narrative poem, *Hiawatha*, about an Indian boy who grows up to be a prophet to his people. Early in the poem, Longfellow describes Hiawatha's attitude toward the animals of the forest.

> Of all beasts he learned the language,
> Learned their names and all their secrets,
> How the beavers built their lodges,
> Where the squirrels hid their acorns,
> How the reindeer ran so swiftly,
> Why the rabbit was so timid,
> Talked with them whene'er he met them,
> Called them Hiawatha's brothers.

Actually, those lines express all Indians' attitude toward wild animals. Indians respected them and depended on them for life itself.

Animals played an important role in their creation myths. In fact, some western Indians believed there had been an Age of Animals before human beings existed. In that age, Old Coyote Man was chief. He was not a totally admirable creature. He was curious and cunning, able to assume many deceptive shapes, gluttonous, and boastful. Yet he was also the creator.

In that long ago time, a great flood occurred. But foresighted Old Coyote Man had built himself an ark. When the rains finally ceased, he hailed two passing ducks and asked them to dive until they found earth. The first duck failed, but the second finally brought some dirt to the surface. From it, Coyote Man created the land, the animals, and the Indians.

In the northeastern Indians' version of the same myth, Glooscap, the Great Hare, is the creator. During the flood, he climbs a pine tree. As the waters rise, he keeps extending the top of the tree. To find earth for a new beginning, he eventually sends the diving animals, otter, beaver, and muskrat, and it is the muskrat who succeeds.

In the Cheyenne version of the same myth (Cheyennes lived in the Great Lakes area), the All Spirit first creates a lake, then water creatures,

and finally birds. It is the coot who dives for the mud, which the All Spirit places on Grandmother Turtle's back to build up Earth. Then Earth becomes the grandmother and brings forth trees, fruits, and flowers. Next, the All Spirit makes man from one of his ribs, and woman from another. Finally, he creates the buffalo so that his people will have food.

The Indians of the Northwest believed that Raven was their creator, fashioning first women and then men from clamshells. He also stole fire from the King of Light to give it to his people.

In another version, Raven changes himself into a cedar leaf and is swallowed in a sip of water by the daughter of the Chief-Who-Had-Light. She becomes pregnant, and her child (Raven in disguise) steals the stars, moon, and sun from his grandfather before flying away.

The Cherokees believed all the animals once lived in darkness, but knew there was light in the East. Possum went first to snatch a bit of light (the sun), but he hid it with his tail and it burned off all his tail fur. Buzzard's attempt wasn't successful either; the sun burned off all his head feathers. But Grandmother Spider was wise; she fashioned some damp clay into a little bowl to carry the light in, and she spun a thread on her way to the East so that she'd know how to get back. Ever since, a spider's web looks like the sun surrounded by rays.

To the Indians, thunder was evidence that the Thunderbirds (powers for goodness) were beating their wings. Their flashing eyes made the lightning. They could destroy or encourage crops as they chose, but generally they were kind to the Indians. The Thunderbirds were often in conflict with the Panthers and Great Horned Snakes who inhabited the Underwater Realm and who were capable of great evil. When the Thunderbirds and the Underwater creatures were in serious conflict, violent storms, floods, and earthquakes occurred. Of course, the conflict also symbolized a struggle between good and evil.

© 1984, 1997 J. Weston Walch, Publisher

Mythology: A Teaching Unit

PART III   WORKSHEET 38

✎ WHAT DO YOU REMEMBER?
WHAT HAVE YOU LEARNED?

- First, let's try matching names and descriptions. Fill in the spaces in Column B with the correct names from Column A. One name may be used twice.

COLUMN A	COLUMN B
Old Coyote Man	1. _____ He succeeded where the beaver and otter had failed.
Raven	2. _____ He was a thief whose stealing helped mankind.
Great Hare	3. _____ The smallest of the diving birds, he was the one who found a bit of earth.
Coot	
Grandmother Spider	4. _____ She was a potter and a spinner.
Muskrat	5. _____ He lost his head feathers.
Grandmother Earth	6. _____ He lost his tail fur.
All Spirit	7. _____ She swallowed a cedar leaf with strange results.
Buzzard	8. _____ They are powers of evil.
Opossum	9. _____ They are generally benefactors to humans.
Thunderbirds	10. _____ He made a great lake.
Great Homed Snakes	11. _____ He climbed an extendable pine tree.
Daughter of the Chief-Who-Had-Light	12. _____ He made women from clamshells.
	13. _____ She produced flowers and trees and fruits.

14. In Indian myths, the porcupine was often a symbol for the sun and the grizzly bear for clouds. Can you see why?

_____

_____

_____

15. Basing your answer on the few myths in this lesson, how would you compare American Indian myths with the Norse? with the Greek? with the African? *Clues:* Which seem the most cheerful to you? In which do the gods seem closest to the people? Which seem most influenced by the natural environment, that is, the place where the people live?

_____

_____

_____

_____

_____

_____

A WABANAKI MYTH

The Wabanaki, "people of the rising sun," lived in what is now eastern Maine, but on hunting expeditions traveled north to Micmac, Maliseet, and even Eskimo territories. Because of Norse occupation of Eskimo lands for many years, their sagas had blended with Eskimo legends. The Wabanaki, familiar with Eskimo myths, also incorporated some Norse characters in their mythology.

Thus Glooskap, their great hero, is dignified, benevolent, noble, and brave—like Thor and Odin in Norse myths. To the Indians, Glooskap represents the good principle. His opposite is Lox the wolf, similar in character to the Norse Loki. He is a devil with mischievous tendencies, as you will find in the following myth where he delights in causing misfortune for the overly trustful Mrs. Bear.

It begins, "Don't live with mean people if you can help it . . . Bad habits get to be devilish second nature. One dead herring is not much, but one by one you can make such a heap of them as to stink out a whole village."

Mrs. Bear, who saw only the best in others, made the mistake of inviting another old woman to live with her. "Their wigwam was all by itself, and the next neighbor was so far off that he was not their neighbor at all, but that of some other folks."

One night the two women settled down to sleep, close to the fire. While they slept, Lox came prowling around and decided to play a trick. He went outside and cut a long pole, then thrust it into the fire until it was red hot. Next, he touched Mrs. Bear's feet with it. She cried out to the other woman, "Take care, you are burning me." Her loud denial was "like a thunderclap."

Lox then played the same trick on the other woman. She dreamed first that the Mohawks were burning her alive, but she soon woke up and accused Mrs. Bear. Then the fight began, and Lox, watching, laughed so hard that he fell down dead with delight.

When the women got up next morning, the dead devil, looking like a raccoon, lay at the door. (He could change shapes at will.) Planning to eat him for breakfast, they skinned him and dropped him into a kettle of boiling water, but it immediately revived him. He leaped out of the kettle, kicked it over into the fire, grabbed his skin off a bush and disappeared into the forest. But his last trick, kicking over the kettle, had caused the ashes to splutter up and blind poor Mrs. Bear.

Now no longer able to hunt or fish or set traps, Mrs. Bear was dependent on the other woman. That one selfishly kept the best food for herself, and Mrs. Bear got only bones and scraps.

Later, when Mrs. Bear was alone, she remembered that the old ones had said a blind person's eyelids might be just stuck, and a clever person could open them again. She took a sharp knife and went to work on her eyelids. Soon she could see as well as ever, but she sad nothing to the other woman.

Mrs. Bear watched as that one cooked the dinner, then set out fine fat venison and fish for herself, filling the "blind" woman's plate only with scraps. At that, Mrs. Bear said sharply, "You have done very well for yourself." Realizing that Mrs. Bear could see, the other was frightened, for Mrs. Bear was by far the "better man of the two," and she hastily explained that she had given Mrs. Bear the wrong dish by accident.

"After that, Mrs. Bear kept her eyes on people in two ways."

✎ A CLOSER LOOK

This myth is different from the others you have read because parts of it (in quotation marks) are the actual words of an Indian storyteller, recorded by Charles B. Leland in a book called *The Algonquin Legends of New England*, published in 1884. The storyteller explained to Leland that his grandfather had told this tale to him when he was a child and that certain parts of it always made him laugh.

• You will remember that some myths were told chiefly to entertain. This one does, but it also teaches because it points out some things about human nature. Let's see if you know what they are.

1. Remember the statement, "One dead herring is not much, but one by one you can make such a heap of them as to stink out a whole village." We have a similar statement, "It takes only one bad apple to spoil a barrel." Both statements are warnings. What is really being said?

   _____

   _____

2. At the end of the story, the narrator says, "After this, Mrs. Bear kept her eyes on people in two ways." Can you explain what the two were? _____

   _____

   _____

3. Why does the narrator say "Mrs. Bear was by far the better man of the two" when he is actually talking about women? What is he implying about Mrs. Bear? _____

   _____

   _____

4. Why do you think the storyteller included the detail that Mrs. Bear's nearest neighbor was so far away that he wasn't really her neighbor at all? In other words, why is the wigwam's isolation important? _____

   _____

   _____

5. Here is a little vocabulary exercise. Check the dictionary for the meaning of the following:

   guileless _____

   credulous _____

   gullible _____

   naive _____

   After you have written the meanings in the space provided, state which adjective best describes Mrs. Bear as the story opens. _____

   What adjective can you supply to describe her after her temporary blindness?

   _____

PART III   LESSON 40

 MYTHS AND RITUALS OF THE PLAINS INDIANS

Among the Native Americans, it was the custom for a boy approaching manhood to undertake some test of endurance to prove himself worthy to be counted among the braves. One such test was to leave the village and go into the forest alone to purify himself by fasting.

As might be expected, fasting sometimes brought about a vision in which a spirit might appear to give the boy instructions, which he was bound to follow. Also as might be expected, the story the boy told when he returned home was sometimes so dramatic that it became a myth. Such a tale was the explanation of how the Indians of the Middle West obtained the gift of corn.

A boy once set out from his village for his sacred trial by fasting. Not having eaten for three days, he was lying weak and hungry on his bed of leaves when a stranger appeared, dressed in green and yellow and adorned with a plume of feathers.

He challenged the boy to a wrestling match, but broke it off after a time, saying he would return the next day. On the second day, the same thing happened. But on the third day, the boy, finding strength he didn't realize he had, overcame the stranger. The stranger acknowledged that the boy had won, but said that they would have to wrestle once more, this time to the death, and if the boy won again, he was to give his opponent proper burial and tend his grave afterward.

On the fourth day of the contest (actually the seventh day of the boy's fast), he was again the victor, and the stranger collapsed and died. The boy buried him carefully and, in the months that followed, returned several times to keep the grave free from weeds.

Finally he returned with his father to the site of his solitary fast. Growing on the stranger's grave were tall slender plants topped with golden ears of corn whose tassels move in the breeze like the stranger's plume of feathers.

The moral of the story was that the boy's privation made him a stronger person and that his triumph over physical weakness resulted in a great benefit for all his people.

◆ ◆ ◆

It was not unusual that a young man's personal trial would be undertaken, not just to prove his own worthiness, but also to appease a god who might then grant a boon to the tribe. Among the Pawnees, young men engaged in ritual self-mutilation to appease the sun god, thus assuring that the crops would flourish. The ritual was the Sun Dance, a test of manhood, but also a sacrifice to the god.

In the dance, a group of young men (sometimes a single man) tied leather thongs to an upright pole. The other end of each thong was tied to a small sharpened stick which was then thrust into a man's chest muscles. The men would circle the pole, always keeping their faces turned toward the sun. Unless the weight of a man's body against the thong or his movements tore the stick from his chest, he was expected to continue the dance until the sun set.

From these two accounts, you can see that the Indians put great emphasis on bravery and courage, but endurance was important as well. All three traits were necessary in a culture where survival depended on a man's ability to cope with a physical environment that was often hostile.

✎ COMING OF AGE, YESTERDAY AND TODAY

• Answer the following questions in the fewest possible words.

1. In your understanding, what was the object of a boy's going into the forest alone to fast?

_____

_____

_____

2. Most teenagers are eager to obtain a driver's license. What does passing the license exam represent to you? _____

_____

3. A legal drinking age and a legal age at which a young man or woman can marry without their parents' consent both exist. Why do you think lawmakers considered it necessary to set these restrictions?

_____

_____

_____

_____

4. How do you define courage? _____

_____

How do you define bravery? _____

_____

Do they mean the same thing to you? _____

Explain. _____

_____

5. In our society, how are teenagers most apt to demonstrate endurance? _____

_____

_____

_____

6. Which would you think was a more difficult trial, the fasting in the forest or the Sun Dance? Explain. _____

_____

_____

_____

PART II'   LESSON 41

TWO INDIAN MYTHS OF THE NORTHWEST

In the previous lesson, you learned how the Plains Indians were introduced to corn, which then became an important part of their diet. Generally, the Indians of the Northwest depended on hunting and fishing to fill their stomachs. But a plant of the lily family, Camas, became a staple food of the Indians in what is now the state of Washington. The legend of Camas is both imaginative and beautiful.

Many years ago, a plague came upon the Indians and threatened to destroy them. The medicine men, determined to save their people, appealed to the Great Chief Above, who promised to send them a savior. Their instruction was to gather at the Place of the Wishing Stone. And so they did, the healthy and the dying, all together.

Just before noon, a medicine man pointed toward the highest mountain on the horizon. As the people stared in amazement, a white light appeared in the sky above it, and out of the light came a beautiful young woman. Slowly she descended until she stood on the Wishing Stone for all to see.

Her message was one of hope. The Great Chief Above had sent her to help them; they had only to touch her to be cured of their malady. At that, the sick people rushed forward and great was their joy to find themselves well once again.

But she had further instructions for them. They must plant the seeds that she would distribute, seeds of the Camas flower. In the spring, the plant would cover the ground with beautiful blue flowers, and in the fall, when it ripened, they were to dig up its roots and eat them. If they did, they would be free of the terrible sickness forever.

When she had given them all the seeds, a breeze lifted her back up into the sky where she disappeared into the clouds. But the people never forgot the spirit of the Camas, and ever after, they left gifts for her on the Wishing Stone where she had stood.

In a society where food gathering occupied much of the people's time, myths were common about the animals which were at once their source of food and their friends. The Indians respected the creatures they had to kill in order to survive. Often they prayed to the spirit of the dead animal, and they never killed needlessly. To do so was a serious offense.

In the Columbia River area, salmon were once so plentiful that the people always had enough to eat, and they even grew fat on the river's bounty. For that bounty, the older people in the tribe were truly grateful. Often they gave thanks to the river spirits as well as the salmon spirits.

Unfortunately, the young men began to take their generous food supply for granted. They were no longer reverent and grateful to the spirits. Even worse, during the spawning season, when the river teemed with salmon, the men caught them, not from need, but just for sport.

Their impiety frightened the older members of the tribe, not without cause; for one day a terrible rumbling was heard, signaling the Great Spirit's anger. Then, as the frightened Indians watched, a great hill erupted in fire. Trees burned, and the river became a river of flame. Most of the people of the village died horribly.

© 1984, 1997 J. Weston Walch, Publisher   82   *Mythology: A Teaching Unit*

Name _____ Date _____

✎ THINKING IT OVER

1. In the first story, the Legend of Camas, what is somewhat unusual about the savior of the people? _____
   _____

2. What is our name for the Indians' Great Chief Above? _____
   _____

3. A white light appeared above the highest mountain. Do you know what white represents symbolically? *Clue:* A bride's gown is generally white.
   _____
   _____

4. Since a plant's roots could cure the sickness, have you any idea what the sickness might have been? _____
   _____

5. What evidence do you have that the Indians in this story were good people? _____
   _____
   _____
   _____

6. It has been said that the Indians were the first conservationists. What evidence is there in the second myth to support that statement? _____
   _____
   _____

7. The myth suggests why the young men became so cruel and indifferent to the life of the salmon. Why so you think they began to behave as they did? _____
   _____
   _____

8. The second myth may have its basis in a natural phenomenon. When it tells of the Great Spirit's way of punishing the people, what is it actually describing? _____
   _____
   _____

PART III **TWO MYTHS FROM THE INDIANS OF THE SOUTHWEST**   LESSON 42

Among the important gods of the Navaho was Spider Woman, who had been instrumental in freeing their land from the monsters that had been threatening them. Her home was Spider Rock, a remarkable sandstone formation in Arizona's Canyon de Chelly National Park.

Despite her kindness to the Navaho, saving them from monsters and teaching them the art of weaving, the Indians used her as a kind of bogey-man, telling their children that if they misbehaved, Spider Woman would carry them to the top of her rock and eat them.

Actually, she was their true benefactress, as one young man discovered. He had been hunting in the canyon when he suddenly realized that he was being stalked by an enemy. Because he was peaceable by nature, he looked around wildly for a way to escape his pursuer.

Spider Rock was just in front of him, but he knew he could never scale it. Then he noticed a strange silk rope hanging down the rock face. Frantically, he tied it around his waist and, using the rope, began his rock climb, leaving his enemy frustrated below.

Once on top, he feasted on eagle's eggs and drank dew to relieve his thirst. Only then did Spider Woman appear, and he realized she had dropped down her web ladder to save him.

Among the Indians, there was a clear division of labor, with the braves hunting to provide the family's meat, and the women curing the hides, tending the gardens, and preparing the food. The following myth suggests that any woman who decides to break with that tradition, no matter how good her reason, is looking for trouble.

A young Zuni girl lived at home with her elderly parents. She had had offers of marriage, but she always refused, for her brothers were dead and no one else was left to take care of the old people. She tended her garden faithfully, but with no hunter in the family, they had no meat. In fact, they were very poor.

One day she boldly told her parents that she herself would go hunting and bring home some fine rabbits. Reluctantly her father outfitted her with a pair of her brothers' deerskin boots and their hunting sticks. Then, bravely, she set out.

With beginner's luck, she bagged four rabbits, treating the dead body of each one with reverence. But so intent was she on her task that before she knew it, she got caught in a snowstorm and lost her way.

She took refuge for the night in a little cave and even made herself a fire. But her troubles were only beginning. Attracted by the fire, a cannibal-demon appeared at the mouth of the cave. Luckily, he was too big to get through the opening.

First, he tried to entice the girl to come outside. When that didn't work, he demanded her rabbits. One by one, she had to throw them to him. So insatiable was his appetite that he demanded her deerskin boots, her blanket, even her dress. When she had nothing more to give, he tried once more to get into the cave, this time using his axe to enlarge the opening.

Fortunately, two gods heard the commotion and came to her rescue, killing the demon. They even cut him open to retrieve her rabbits and her clothing. They also gave her some advice, saying that it was unwise for a woman to try to do a man's work. Instead, she should get married and let her husband do the hunting. She took their advice to heart, and when she was safely back home, she married the first young man who asked her.

© 1984, 1997 J. Weston Walch, Publisher   84   *Mythology: A Teaching Unit*

✎ WORDS AND MEANINGS

entice   insatiable   refuge   retrieve

- First, let's try a little vocabulary quiz, based on the words in today's lesson. Choose the correct word from the list above to fill in the blank in each of the following sentences.

1. So _____ was Odin's thirst for knowledge that he was willing to make self-sacrifices, if by doing so, he could learn more.

2. When we went boating on the river, I dropped my hat overboard. Despite several tries, we couldn't _____ it.

3. The Pied Piper of Hamlin was able to _____ their village because they wanted to follow his music.

4. The hunted man took _____ in a church, believing that he would be safe there.

- Now let's take a closer look at today's stories. Answer the following questions in the fewest possible words.

5. In warning their children that Spider Woman would take them to the top of her rock and eat them if they misbehaved, what were the Indians probably trying to discourage the children from doing? _____

   _____

   _____

6. The young man who is saved by Spider Woman is quick-thinking and resourceful. Does he fit the pattern of earlier heroes you have met in the myths? Explain. _____

   _____

   _____

7. State briefly the moral of the story of the Zuni girl who wanted to be a hunter.

   _____

   _____

   _____

8. Do you agree with the message in this myth? Explain. _____

   _____

   _____

9. What attitude toward the elderly is expressed in this myth? _____

   _____

   _____

   _____

PART III   ✎ TEST III   LESSON 43

• In this test, you will be asked to remember some details from the lessons you have studied, but you will also be asked to comment on the significance of some of the stories you have read, and as always, you will have a few questions that deal with vocabulary words you have learned in your reading.

Let's start with a matching game. Match the character in Column A with the description in Column B. You will note that the characters are listed under their place of origin. Good luck!

COLUMN A   COLUMN B

From Africa

1. **Anansi**   _____ wanted to become a storyteller

2. **Hare**   _____ a wizard and a trickster

3. **Hyena**   _____ symbol of royalty

4. **Snake**   _____ taught the Navaho to weave

5. **Nkoyo**   _____ powers for goodness

6. **Number Eleven**   _____ in this country, Br'er Rabbit

7. **Yiyi**   _____ refused the suitors her father chose

From the United States   _____ the Prometheus of the animal kingdom; brought fire to earth

8. **Glooscap**   _____ outsmarted Death

9. **Grandmother Spider**   _____ in time of flood, built himself an ark

10. **Lox**   _____ the Great Hare, the Creator

11. **Old Coyote Man**   _____ snatched a bit of light from the sun

12. **Spider Woman**   _____ a wolf-devil

13. **Sun Dancers**   _____ those who perform self-sacrifice by self- mutilation

14. **Thunderbirds**

15. In Africa, why do people wear animal masks? _____

16. What was the Indians' attitude toward the animals and fish they killed for food?

_____

_____

17. In the story of Nkoyo, what was the cause of her troubles?

_____

_____

_____

18. What is the moral of the story of the Zuni girl who wanted to be a hunter?

_____

_____

_____

19. In the Wabanaki myth, in what way was Mrs. Bear not careful enough?

_____

_____

_____

20. What was the fault of the other woman in the story of Mrs. Bear?

_____

_____

_____

21. Why did young Indian males engage in a test of strength and endurance?

_____

_____

_____

ingenunity   voracious   gullible   entice   impiety

• Choose a word from the list above to complete each of the sentences below.

22. The _____ of the young salmon fishermen brought disaster to their village.

23. The cannibal-demon had such a _____ appetite that he even ate cloth.

24. Odysseus's _____ enabled him to get out of some very difficult situations unharmed.

25. Poor Mrs. Bear was so _____ that others could take advantage of her.

26. Because the invalid's appetite was poor, the cook tried to think of special foods that would

_____ him to eat.

SUMMING UP

At the beginning of this course, you were told that myths are like a museum of the mind, that they enable us to know how people thought long ago. They let us see those human beings as fearful or cheerful, generous or mean, cruel or merciful, wise or foolish—in short, as people with the same virtues and faults that we have.

But myths enable us to see something even more remarkable: that people living in widely separated areas and times, people who apparently had no contact with each other, produced similar myths.

Some force created an ordered universe—whether it was Eros, the Greek principle of order; the All Spirit of the American Indian; or God.

Whether we read of Hades, Hel and Valhalla, or heaven and hell, the mythic concept of an afterlife included some sort of reward and punishment.

Pandora opened the box, and Eve plucked the apple. Either story was an explanation of how evil came into the world.

Deucalian and Pyrrha, Noah, and Old Coyote Man all survived a great flood by building an ark. Each of their stories served as a reassurance that human beings would survive, even though Nature, at times, seemed determined to destroy them.

Each hero went through an initiation rite to prove himself. Hercules killed the snakes; Theseus moved the boulder to get the sword and sandals; Arthur pulled the sword from the stone. A quest was part of each hero's life, too. Perseus's was to secure the head of Medusa; Arthur's knights went in search of the Holy Grail. One quest was physical; the other, spiritual. Finally, the heroes Apollo, Hercules, and Odysseus descended into the darkness of the Underworld, then returned to light and life. They were resurrected, as was Jesus. Thus, all defeated death.

It could be said that each hero is an archetype. That is, he represents a universal model of the ideal toward which other people strive. A variety of archetypes exist in the myths. We recognize them and give them the same symbolic signifi-

cance as did people long ago. Thus, the snake represents evil, and the lamb, innocence. For example, if we see a painting of a seemingly peaceful scene where the artist shows a snake lurking in a corner, we fantasize a sequel to the scene in which evil and destructive forces take over. The artist has brought out the same reaction in us that he did in his contemporaries because he used a universal symbol.

Universal symbols are at work, not only during our conscious hours, but also in our dreams. We wake up screaming, certain that a monster is about to overtake us; we are pursued and "freeze in our tracks," or we try to scream and no sound comes. Such recurring dreams are so common that "dream books" have been written, listing all the symbolic figures that trouble our sleep and attempting to show what they represent or foretell. Of course, dreams are not always unpleasant. Sometimes in dreams we accomplish feats that would be impossible in the daytime; for dreams, like myths, encompass our aims, our beliefs, and our fears.

Swiss psychiatrist Carl Jung studied dreams and came to a remarkable conclusion. First, dreams can be divided according to content. The most common simply reflect or distort the day's happenings and are easily accounted for. Certain recurring dreams, such as the sensation of falling, reflect the individual's concerns or fears. Others reflect the concerns or values of society.

Jung believed we go beyond all such dreams as these and find, in other dreams, recurring symbols or motifs that we have inherited from our human past, universal memories common to all people in all places. These make up what Jung termed the "collective unconscious." Jung's idea accounts for similar myths appearing in ancient societies located far apart from each other. Of course, the Eastern myths could have spread through Europe as people migrated or traded, but how about their parallels in the American Indian myths? The concept of a universal (archetypal) memory might be the answer.

✎ LET'S TRY SOME WORD ASSOCIATIONS

- First, let's test your reaction to some of these universal symbols. Just write the first thing that comes to your mind when you see the following words.

1. **snake** _____
2. **lamb** _____
3. **toad** _____
4. **lion** _____
5. **mule** _____
6. **owl** _____
7. **eagle** _____
8. **the color red** _____
9. **the color yellow** _____
10. **the color black** _____

- When you finish, compare your answers with those of your classmates.

  Did you see the toad, like the snake, as evil? In some myths it is, luring animals and people to destruction. In others, it guards knowledge or symbolizes moneymaking. Like other universal symbols, then, it may have good or bad aspects.

  In one of the myths, you have already met the centaur Nessus. A centaur had the head, arms, and upper torso of a man, but the body and legs of a horse. Griffins, in the myths, were creatures with bodies like lions, and heads and wings like eagles.

  The god Pan had the body of a man, a crooked, flattened nose, and the ears, horns, legs, and tail of a goat, as did the satyrs, the masculine followers of Dionysus.

11. What do you think was the significance of the human-animal combinations of

    A. the centaurs _____

    _____

    B. Pan and the satyrs _____

    _____

12. What was the significance of the lion-eagle combination of the griffins?

    _____

    _____